IF YOU WANT

You can

FLY

Rossana Condoleo

I0616373

DISCLAIMER AND COPYRIGHT

IF YOU WANT YOU CAN FLY
An Inspirational and Motivational Book, Coaching Single Moms & Dads in their Quest for Love, Happiness and Fulfilling Relationships
Author: © 2017 Rossana Condoleo
Copy-Editing: The Pedantic Punctuator
Book Cover and Interior Design: © 2017 Rossana Condoleo
Illustration: Copyright © Shutterstock Inc. - Mrs. Opossum

Requests to publish work from this book should be sent to:
Rossana@RossanaCondoleo.com

Published by Rossana Condoleo www.rossanacondoleo.com

ISBN-13 978-3-947120-91-8 (Paperback 6x9 inches)
Also available as eBook

IF YOU WANT

You can

FLY

An Inspirational and Motivational Book, Coaching Single Moms & Dads in their Quest for Love, Happiness and Fulfilling Relationships

Rossana Condoleo

CONTENTS

This book is dedicated...

...to my Reader

Yes, because you deserve it! You have picked me as your guide and mentor for flying to new Love, Relationships and Happiness Destinations... inside and outside yourself. That makes you special to my eyes and even more to my heart. By doing so you have given me love and I will return this love to you from here on.

Thank you!

Rossana Condoleo

DO YOU KNOW? - We have just started walking side-by-side and you have already activated a wonderful virtuous circle!

1 JUST BETWEEN US

Did you ever finish the toilet tissue and repeatedly look at the empty roll while having to grasp for an alternative? It looks back at you, sarcastically reminding you: *"Oh God, how miserable your life is! You don´t even have the time to go and shop for new toilet paper!"* You must be a top-manager without a maid, or a single mom/dad. In the last instance you would never postpone replenishing the contents of your fridge with all your children's needs, I can put my hand on fire on it!

If I ever write my memoirs, I'll need three volumes to tell my entire story. This is why each time I start to talk about myself in written form, I stop almost immediately; it's also one of the two reasons why you find almost no personal information about me on the internet or anywhere else (the second being *Privacy Protection*). The heavy load of events, problems, restrictions and limitations I had and still have to deal with from the past fifteen years (since I moved abroad to marry and divorce from what was to become the most negative person in my past, present, and future life) is just overwhelming. But I never like to entertain myself or my readers with my personal dramas, at least, not my private ones. Instead, I'd like to share the way I really see my life… infinitely brighter than it really is, and help you understand how you can grasp so much inner happiness and balance, that you won´t need anything except your increased inner strength to cope with whatever life and other people throw at you. The advice, ideas and practices you're going to read and learn, have been used by myself to make me strong, *rock-like;* and those strengths are the same ones I've passed on to the people I've motivated and inspired so far, both personally and through my writings.

I am very romantic and sensitive, to the point where I've written more than six hundred poems in my early life (some of which have been collected and published). However, in my capacity as a life-coach, for example in this book, it is my sense of humor which takes the stage. My personal style reveals that despite my life sometimes being overly-difficult, I am at peace with myself and can smile and be happy to the point of infecting many others with happiness. It is truly possible to transform our lives for the better, independently from whatever problems befall us. Some embrace religious beliefs and pray to gods to sustain their hopes and fulfill their need of security, a security which slips away from us many times each week… in fact, far too many days each year…

Eventually, we come to the obvious conclusion that life is, more often than not, *something that can't be wished or prayed for.* You need no God other than yourself to feel grounded, strong, whole, balanced, and happy. As a matter of fact, everyone can become his/her own 'Home', the one most people around the world are unsuccessfully seeking from other places and other people. It is, indeed, inside us: it is portable and cozy and most of all, nobody can take it away.

Now, if coping with life is not an easy task for everyone, at certain stages – at least for a single parent – it becomes a daily act of heroism. I am a big provider, both financially and emotionally;

someone who undertakes huge responsibilities, and I blame myself for being like that – because my life would be a lot easier if I could only spend more time centering myself. Almost all single parents are providing more, both financially and emotionally, than average parents do for their children. Among other things, we feel a need to compensate for what our children do not have and enjoy: two parents together – a complete family. Even when our children are happy with their situation (which we take to mean never 'fully happy'), we still feel that we need to do whatever we can to help them overcome what we see as missing *normality*. That's why most single parents are overwhelmed by balancing work life and exclusive, twenty four hours a day caregiving: matching children's timetables/accidents/problems with a full time job requires a high degree of mastery if you want to keep your job!

I can't guarantee you that you'll start controlling your life more capably after reading and practicing with me and my book, but I promise you that you'll feel a lot more fulfilled in yourself by assimilating and following my advice. This is about happiness, love, dating, relationships, and self-development; how to cope with problems, become and find the right partner for life, becoming more self-confident and lots, lots more. It is a 'pleasant, uplifting read', my readers tell me. It also contains six coaching exercises (most of them with multiple tasks to complete) which really help – believe me – to get a handle on your life, and help prepare you as a prospective partner.

The children? They're in here too, don't worry. We could never forget about them, even if we wanted to! But in my book *YOU* are the very center of my attention and care. They will enjoy having a happy mom or dad, instead of dealing with a sad face to eat dinner with. Now, let me wish you a successful and constructive future, filled with happiness and love!

2 HAPPY INSIDE 24/7

Happiness Inside, is a central life principle; it's important in granting self-stability and HD (*High Definition*) experiences at all times, as well as continuity of purposes - especially on the brink of changes.

"*Happiness supports enthusiasm and empowers creativity and initiative.*
Happiness makes you a better person in your private, family, and work spheres.
Happiness keeps you healthy and lets you stick to your plans.
You have to cultivate happiness as if it were the most precious flower in your garden."

"*Do the things you like to be happier, stronger and more successful. Only so is hard work replaced by dedication.*"

- From **HAPPY DIVORCE**, by Rossana Condoleo.

You will experience bad days, but they won't consume your life. Some simple universal truths, like happiness, come to people through different methods. Some are based on statistical data, sampled during decades of hard work and experimentation. Others are the result of pure inspiration, a communication channel with the universe, starting at the intersection between our true self and a genuine and authentic desire to be part of the whole. Am I religious? Nope! I accept anything, which brings my senses, my brain, and my heart to new levels of experience and understanding. As we grow old, we might learn that we never stop learning. Recently I have entered a new level of awareness, just like in PC games! It is exciting and stimulating, although it might hurt at times. Some experiences can be devastating, such parting from a loved one or divorcing… and yet they offer the substance, the essential matter for growing and improving ourselves. We are not so naïve as to expect that the world turns entirely good because we have decided to be happy, are we? And yet, we will do everything within our power, we will be so dedicated to the search for happiness, that we will be able to not only contain the damages, but also to win over any kind of adversity!

Happiness starts with a simple statement:
"I WANT TO BE HAPPY."

2.1 EASING EMOTIONAL PAIN

I am happy... not in every moment of the day, but generally I can say I'm happy! Feeling emotional pain is good, as long as it's only experienced for limited periods of time. Sometimes we grow closer to other people through pain. We become more sensitive. We are able to be artistic while feeling pain. It is also true that dramas have to be filtered and purified through pain, for us to move past them in a healthy manner. If you feel that you want to cry because you have lost your job, you should do it. If you want to vent the emotions in your heart, do it! If, at the moment, you are unable to see the light at the end of the tunnel, please, let the volcano erupt... it will be a cleansing experience, and soothing! But be ready to be strong in a day or two; don't let yourself be captured and strangled by pain.

Use pain, don't let pain use you! And smile, even while feeling the pain. "My life is so big, and I am so strong, and powerful, and happy, that I can overcome any pain!"

As soon as you fall down into a well of pain, and the ground becomes too cold, look at yourself from outside of your body, let your sense of compassion activate for the friend who is lying there; the best friend you have always had and the best friend you will ever have. It is you! And...

You have to hug your person on the ground,
offer your hand for them to stand up and
start separating each aspect of the drama
from the dramatic scene as a whole.

In the last years I have learnt the most precious lesson of my life, and I bring it to you:

LOVE wipes out every pain!

Right when the werewolf in you is screaming at its loudest, you must sense and feel the universal love; love for the people who made you suffer, love for your children, for your parents, for your colleagues, for your friends, love for the things at hand… nature, the elements (water, fire, wind and air)… for life itself!

Go outside, look at the sky and search for
the sun. Let yourself be inundated with its
empowering light. Is it a cloudy day?
No, problem… tomorrow, it won't be!

Love, Experience and Appreciate is my paradigm; "Nothing and no one can take my happiness away!"

2.2 THE ONE-PROBLEM SYSTEM

If you look at a problem as a *single* problem, you will be able to tackle it by deploying all your positive attitude and problem solving abilities. If you think of all your problems as a system of bad omens plaguing your life, it will be more difficult for you to be really discerning and objective.

Consider and solve *one problem at a time*, and while doing so, ignore the others. I know that sometimes, problems will be connected to one another; but please, as far as it is possible, analyse the situation containing an individual problem, and combine all of your senses to finding a solution. Be creative. Be open to and evaluate any external suggestions, from whatever sources which might help you solve that individual problem. SMILE, as this is only *one problem*!

> As soon as a black cloud named 'THE PROBLEMS' stops over your head, lower your gaze away from it, and focus on the 'ONE PROBLEM' you are tackling right now.

You can also put aside any individual 'one problem' for a while; for example, while waiting for third parties to offer their input; or for other elements to enter the equation, which in turn, help to reach a suitable solution. Then you can take the next 'one problem' and focus on that one, exclusively. And so on…

Solve 'one problem' at a time!

I would ask that you please treat what I am going to say with caution. The meaning you might take from it immediately, isn't the true nature of the concept.

Problems are only problems, for as long as you consider them as such!

What exactly is a problem? Wikipedia offers this definition in their list of examples: "*In business and engineering, a problem is often defined as a difference between actual conditions and those that are required or desired.*"

Simply put, it means:

If I lower my expectations regarding the results/solution, I will diminish the ability of the problem to seem so overwhelming.

It also means that:

If I don't mentally think of it as the 'problem at hand', it will lose its momentum as a problem.

It also means that:

If I consider the issue at hand as being not a problem, but as a special task, I am more compelled to accomplish it.

This turns into activating yourself – whether using your grey brain substance or available resources, it is not important –what is important is that you have started to react (emotionally) and act (move forward).

What we desire is important and we must put our wishes at the top of our list of thoughts, every single day. What we receive should not be so distant or different from what we wish for, in the long run.

We can compromise up to a certain extent! However, the truth is, if we let other people abuse our hopes and dreams, which is the

*place where our life projects are created, we
give them the key to our happiness.*

Remember this when you meet a new special person and he/she is asking you renounce any of your hopes and dreams, life projects included. Compromise is good, and it's needed to initiate, stay and remain in a harmonious, fulfilling and loving relationship, however…

*Whatever feels as if it is 'too much'" and
perceived in your mind as 'too much' in a
relationship, must be revised and corrected.
ASAP!*

Back to the *One Problem = One-Task theory*… I now have to deal with a task – I will no longer consider it a problem! Here are some examples:

- The task of earning more money.
- The task of creating a pleasant relationship with my awkward neighbour.
- The task of understanding that my child is going through a difficult time (puberty, college, divorce, etc.) and I need to change how I offer my help, if I want to be helpful.
- The task of keeping my home clean, without employing cleaners or wasting my free time.

And so on… Of course, loving relationships present a certain number of *tasks*!

Think of a PROBLEM as BLACK
One Problem = One Task.
Think of a TASK as YELLOW

"TASK is a positive concept.
After the task is accomplished, I will have
acquired something which didn't exist before.
I am a creator!"

Visualize one BLACK problem, and then switch your mind to 'Task Mode' and observe the problem gradually changing colour from black into a bright yellow.

2.3 THE EXPERIENCE BOOK

We can learn from problems and pain. They can be life changing. The size of these life changes depends on the number of similar experiences we undertake before we begin to understand that because it was painful, it would be safer and cleverer not to replicate the experience again. Learning how to detect a problem before it enters our *vital area* (military definition) is critical!

Be it a new puppy, a prospective friend, a possible lover, or a fresh job, you must mentally check your own experiences book, to discover if you have gone through a similar life situation with unpleasant outcomes.

An example: when grocery shopping with my daughter, she often suggests we purchase something she has repeatedly expressed a dislike for - leaving it untouched on the table. In my role as both mother and financier, I need to keep these past experiences in mind, and prevent my daughter from putting something in the shopping cart merely because *'it looks so tasty!'* Items that appear attractive don't always taste good! There are people who regularly forget what it means to be responsible for a pet (cleaning, walking, healthcare, spending time with the animal). They also forget that a puppy will cheerfully urinate all over the floor / sofa / furniture / carpet / hi-fi before learning to do it at the designated time and place. It is the same with people. They will not urinate on your floor, but they will sometimes display aspects of their personality which clash with yours… and you sense it, because you have already experienced similar issues in the past! There is possibly more than one entry of this kind in your Experience Book if you choose to be frank with yourself. But please, pay a lot of attention to how you use this book, since…

Checking the Experience Book is a skill!
Be wise enough not to put any New
Experience under a microscope.

There is no better way to reduce the
sensation, the beauty, the possibilities, the
intensity and the promise of a new reality
(be it an object, a person, an animal, a plant
or a new concept) than by abnormally
observing it.
And if you do so, you might completely lose
touch with what is happening around you.

Sometimes, the atmosphere between two people who are getting to know each other on their first date chills down to freezing point; the reason is often imparting too much observation and self-control. The Experience Book lays at the side of Mr. Possibly Right and Ms. Might Be Right, and it is *Ice at first sight*! While there might be a second meeting, or a third, what happened during the first date is likely to create an imprint on the following meetings and you will need to work very hard to repair the damage. I will come back to this point.

2.4 RISK TAKING AND FAILURES

Never be afraid of failures; they are part of the game. You optimize and harmonize your reality, but the target is not perfection...
it is happiness!

Let us have a look at a number of qualities and their respective heat temperatures:

- Perfection is aseptic, white, static and cold. It's often an extreme expression of self-love.
- Happiness is sentimental, multi-coloured, warm, lively, and dynamic – crowded with universal love.

BE OPEN TO new thoughts, to new people, to new principles, to new ideas, to new experiences. 'NEW' MAKES US GROW!

Be open to the prospect of entering new territories and undertaking new and exciting experiences. Accept also, that there is a certain component of risk in all your endeavours... Find a balance with what you have learnt from your experiences – which is an ability we share with other primates, such as chimpanzees, and makes us different from most other animal species. Nature continually selects and improves through experience, developing new features and skills, both in the animal and plant world.

There is no improvement without experience,

and no experience without risk!

2.5 DEPENDENT RELATIONSHIPS AKA, ENERGY SUCKERS

I will tell you a story. It is about my past propensity towards accepting 'dependent relationships'. Until the time when I finally looked into my own *Experience Book*, and realized that for most of my life I was being *consumed*, not loved as a friend. This truth is not absolute, because I do indeed have some really loving friends...but *the majority creates the rule*!

The essence of a dependent relationship is that it is parasitic in nature; where the dependent person uses their host like a tick uses an animal. After sucking all the life energy they require, they leave the host and run a transient self-standing life up until they reach exhaustion. Then, they jump onto another host for refilling with fresh life-energy.

Barbie (which is a fictional name) was a fake-blond, doe-eyed medical student, with a sparkling life concept and a supernatural memory; she could learn the entire anatomy book in one week and pass the exam with honours! With this energy-sucker, it was love at first sight. She started to dance with me at a party, despite the fact that I was accompanied by my fiancée. We were both open, original and we became close friends almost instantly. I often invited her to go out, even when I was meeting my boyfriend alone. And she was perfect; she never attempted to lure the attention of my good looking mate away from me.

I was too much in love with my new close friend Barbie, to realize that the friendship was becoming *disturbing*... for me! She was dating any boy who would offer her a compliment. I tried to open her eyes to this situation, in an attempt to prevent her from being disillusioned over and over again. But, punctually and without fail, she came to me in the middle of the night, crying desperately, because each one had treated her so badly! She suffered insomnia issues, due to these continually poor relationship choices.

Sometimes she caught two buses, just to come to my place and sleep with me... in my single bed! For Barbie, I was the equivalent of a soothing cup of chamomile tea, a nurturing mother, and in Barbie's mind, the source of her inner balance. But no one can be the source of our own personal balance. That must always stay and remain inside us, in the centre of our own body.

Take responsibility for your inner happiness!

I knew what I wanted, pretty well most of the time, while Barbie was still on the quest for her own essence. And in her situation, it was a very chaotic search. The task for me, was to point her attention towards her repeated mistakes with men, and try to get her to focus on the need to learn from experience.

I was really at the end of my tether with Barbie… After warning her for what was probably the tenth (or twentieth) time that the 'new' guy was going to make her unhappy, she would ignore me (her right!) and soak up the guy's promise of endless love.

When it all fell apart, she would also drink a lot of alcohol to forget him, as usual. There was no way of compromising with such a wild creature… she sucked away my time; for talking; for checking her clothes and hairstyle before dating; for explanations about her medical exams; for improving her relationships with her big brother and her father; and for calming her mother over the phone, assuring her nothing bad was going to happen while Barbie was with me; for cleaning the floor after she'd vomited (hangovers)! And so on and so forth. I told her I couldn't guarantee her that level of *total support* in the long run; I had a life of my own, which was also a very busy one! But she didn't change her parasitic attitude. Not even a little bit.

And what about me? She hardly listened to my own problems, if at all! She diverted the conversation back to herself at every opportunity.

Realizing that this relationship was not healthy, that Barbie was, in fact, an energy-sucker, I had to leave her behind me. She reacted with anger, and criticized me. I did think she could at least be thankful for my Bed and Breakfast services!

There always comes a time when energy-suckers come to the realization that they've been dependent — and they don't like it.
Not at all!

The energy-suckers defence mechanisms activate against their host, and the host becomes a fiend, rather than a saviour. Ego problems are at the basis of this issue and I have learned, through experience, to detect someone who has ego problems at first sight. It is my choice then, whether I want to start a relationship with that person; I am aware of the special effort it requires, and I am prepared to quit if their neediness overwhelms me.

Declare to yourself...

"I want to be loved — not consumed."

Energy-suckers are found everywhere - among business partners, colleagues, in your own family, and online.

Practice regular decluttering operations, to ensure that the people gravitating around you are worth your love, time and availability.

Later on, I will give you a simple, amusing trick you can use, to detect the best people to accept into your life – to preserve and accrue even more happiness.

Single parents have to economize their mental and emotional resources, to optimize their results on the job and in the family.

We are required to multitask in absence of an important energy source: a partner for life and a heat for the nights! The heat of a body we trust and love, not one belonging to a casual encounter, is an important source of self-confidence and inner stability. We have to compensate for this lack with extra life energy of our own.

"I am myself! I alternate stress with fun and maintain a balanced, give-and-take in my life-energy account."
This is 'The Economics of Self' according to Rossana Condoleo

Have you detected an energy-sucker in your life? Modify, adjust and eliminate what is required, following your own criteria for personal balance, harmony and happiness.

Happiness starts by loving yourself and life.
Celebrate yourself, and celebrate your life,
each and every single day!

2.6 HELPING PEOPLE TO BE HAPPY

Being giving is a big quality.
Being too giving is a big mistake!

Overdoing this aspect of your personality, by giving too much, might produce disorders in your own balance (see previous chapter). But...

Being helpful and loving is one of the basic
rules of nature!
Giving with generosity, with a good heart,
without expecting anything in return; this is
an enriching event in itself.

What to give?

- *Availability:* Giving your time for being there, with a person or group of people who need you.
- *Advice:* If you feel you can say any words of wisdom, which are likely to help wipe dark clouds away from another person's sky.
- *Playfulness:* Your sense of humour may be helpful to others, by making people smile.

- *Initiatives:* Offer actions and practical help.

- *Money donations:* Help out charitable institutions; and if you can, diversify, so that more institutions and people can benefit from your efforts. Remember, also, that even one dollar a year is okay. If it makes you happy – you should do it!

- *Your own happiness:* Share it, find pictures or phrases which touch people and let them think. Tell stories about your happiness.

- *Love:* In all its forms, from words of praise, through to words expressing your feelings to others, and remembering things about your beloved ones and celebrating their important dates. Try to go out of your way to be loving and to help other people feel special, because this is the basis of your own happiness!

   Very important:

*Service starts in the family!
Be sure you have helped your children and
your future partner to be happy, and then
enlarge the radius of your generosity outside
your nucleus.*

Happiness is a life plan, a system of light shining principles which, after you learn them, become an integral part of your own beliefs.

No efforts will be needed afterwards, to be happy on a regular twenty-four-hour basis.

I have learnt a lot of things about myself while helping others! *Learning by teaching.* Another positive side effect is that you simply realize your life is wonderful, in comparison to those of other people. In fact, among the thousands of human beings who are starving on a daily basis, or perhaps dying from a rare illnesses and with whom you hardly can relate and connect, there are normal people – like you – who are experiencing the same situations, but at a much higher level of difficulty. The sort of situations *likely to drive you insane,* have the strongest positive impact on your *emotional immune system*; you can start to react and act with a strength and power never seen and never imagined before… Or you can opt out and let this mega-power become self-annihilating. It's up to you!

Teach people how it works, help them achieve happiness and a fulfilling life! When you offer to help, don't expect people to listen or to do what you propose. Example: You watch your ninety-year old neighbour who is still mowing their own grass once a week. You come outdoors with your PC Tablet, jump over the fence, and let him see a variety of convenient mowing robots available on the internet. The old man kindly refuses your suggestion however; because he is convinced that mowing the grass is the secret to his longevity! Don't be discouraged, not all the attempts to be of help will hit the target.

The fact that people may want to solve their own problems, or their unhappiness on their own, is a decision which you need to respect.

And...

Never tell a mom how she should raise her children and give no advice regarding their schooling, health or nutrition unless you are asked.

2.7 ACTIVITY AND POISE

Happy people are always engaged in something interesting, either for themselves, or for others.

Taking four hours to yourself, for your own wellbeing at a spa, is being active. Meditation is an activity. Taking your colleagues to enjoy a beer, is an activity. Taking a break and flying to the Fiji Islands is an activity.

Inactivity is sitting five hours before the TV, or chatting indefinitely over the phone or on your social networks, or indefinitely postponing activities. Time is also an issue – we need to take responsibility for our time and that of our children, because we have not got endless amounts of it. Every minute is a minute less that we have left until the X day!

Find a balance between the concept of 'Life is a wild river, it flows like it flows' and 'Life is a Plan'.

I am for action, and action is for me Life itself. No Action = No Life. But... overdoing is always a mistake, and there are times when you have to simply let time work for you and be patient...

Time creates. Let time work at your projects.

And...

Let your projects develop their own beautiful architecture.

If you are a starter, a mover, a provider, a friend of your family, of yourself and mankind – then you don't have to feel overwhelmed by action at all costs. Pretending to control the multiplicity and variety, as well as the complexity of our world, is utopia. We have to allow ourselves time to be just what we are: wonderful human beings. The majority of us will be able to find a compromise between giving ourselves time to just 'be', and the demands we are confronted with daily, at work, within the family and within our friend network.

Most leaders are poised, but not all poised individuals are leaders. Whether these leaders learned to be poised, or they are poised from birth, is not important. Behind their poise, is there the substance of a leader? Give yourself the answer. Those who don't want or need to be leaders, and merely want to be charismatic and attract lot of followers, create a *poise for themselves*. Politicians work a lot in this regard, especially when they are *on display*.

Then, if religious, business, politics, and social leaders are poised, it must be that they think deeply and let time go. They stop the world.

They say... "Hey, wait a minute dude... I am pondering!"

Whenever there is a situation which is pressuring you, be it presented by your children, or by your boss, or whoever else thinks his interest comes before yours – take your time. Everybody has their own inner time schedule. I am hectic and punctual and I cannot present as being poised if I know I'm running late. My daughter is tranquillity personified. Nobody is able to accelerate her personal rhythm, through which she achieves brilliant results. I'm not in a position to transfer my own hectic feelings on to her - even though I would like her to be *faster* and I am at the point of yelling at her, especially in the morning before school time. Her face remains calm and collected, and she is sweet; she remains gracious in her movements... she is naturally poised! With her volcanic mom, my daughter succeeds in protecting her own world. She allows nobody to disrupt the integrity of her core. I understand there is absolutely no pettiness involved in her refusal to change her speed... it is nature at work, protecting individuality.

But what if everyone in the world were poised and nobody was exuberant and boisterous, displaying emotional ups and downs?

There are countries, such as Malaysia, where all people are culturally poised. In front of

39

any obstacle or evil, they preserve their calm
and portray the presence of the control they
need to avoid energy dips in useless internal
or external conflicts.
Conflict is inevitable, and the parties accept,
from the very beginning and with poise, that
there will be one loser and one winner.

2.8 ACCEPTING WHAT IT IS

I persevere to the point of being stubborn at times; it is my warrior soul, *and* my Achilles' heel! But I am improving this aspect of my character... and the more I learn to accept what it is, the more I am happy with my life. A relationship breakup, a project, which is no longer sustained by your department, a person who fails to respond to your expectations, a chronic illness, for example, are all areas in which perseverance is good, but there comes a time when you need to step back.

> *The warrior must prevail and fight, but not at the cost of his own life! There's a time when a white flag must necessarily signal Surrender.*

Is this capitulation, or is it merely surrendering to the evidence of one's limited power within the universal order of things? If it was not so, we would be able to control whatever falls under our spectrum of interests... from our loved ones, to colleagues, and even nature. Why not? But... is it really the world that you want? No surprises, no excitement, a situation where everything is planned and falls right into place?

What we are doing on this planet is accomplishing exactly the same life cycle as every other living being on earth, mosquitos included. We are just as vulnerable as a mosquito, maybe even more so! By connecting with nature and its simple laws, paradoxically, we stop being afraid of death. Important things must be said at least thrice to be acknowledged; and this concept deserves it! Some years ago, I was greatly in need of an antidote to my lack of religious faith and the consequent hopelessness arising vis-à-vis life after death. I became more aware of my position in the universe. I realized how small, and how big I am. And still I have no idea of what comes after death. I am no longer asking myself questions regarding this subject. I am content with the life I have, with the time I have, and too busy with them both to engage in metaphysical thoughts about life-after-death!

That's it! *Accepting what it is*, is the same thing!

We live constantly on the borderline between the field of life and that of death. We are, really, always in the middle! Think about your matter; which is made of flesh, not iron. Flesh, not metastable allotropes of carbon i.e. diamonds. Flesh, not plastic… just flesh. I get really angry observing a plastic pen and realizing that in 200 years it will be still be here, while my own life expectation is only 150 years (it was 115, but I raised it recently!). What do you need to reach the other field? Nothing! Cross the road without looking left, then right and left again and you could get hit by a car! There are some interesting, but possibly dangerous red berries in my garden. If I want to go to heaven, I just have to eat more than a couple of them, and I'm done!

The potential early loss of your life should also give you heightened awareness of the passage of time, of a life which is too short to be lost behind objectively impossible undertakings.

I'm the first to dream big and to stretch above and beyond my actual possibilities. But…

Be it in your love life or at work, when you are running low on life energies, raise your white flag and relax. It really is time to be calm… to be silent and absorb and reflect the light and the love around you.
You don't always need to replace something which is gone!
Let it go, and allow life to surprise you with its blessings!

2.9 KEEPING IN TOUCH WITH YOURSELF AND YOUR WISHES

As situations change around us, we change accordingly, or conversely, we change and our space changes. It is normal that these interactions between yourself and the realities around you are continual. So, don't be surprised if at a certain point, you no longer like French fries, or your job grows uninteresting, or there is a growing distance between your closest friends and you. In fact, no matter how badly we try to stick to the old – because it's comfortable, reassuring and warm – change affects relationships also. It's not important whether this change is for good or bad, because all people change, too. What happens in the meantime, is reciprocal fine-tuning – in order to fit the level of relationship we used to have with someone originally, who in the meantime, like it or not, has taken different life directions. We can still be kind to each other, but intimacy, that feeling of deeply understanding each other, might have disappeared. To be happy it's essential to accept change as a matter of fact, as a law of nature!

Don't be afraid of change, since change brings about maturity and development. For a plant to grow bigger, repotting is needed!

Responding to change means using imagination, creativity and putting ideas into motion. The process requires three steps:

1. Adapt – When all your efforts are focused on understanding a new reality, and you make changes inside yourself, to fit into it.

2. React – When you are totally *inside* the new reality, you are aware of it, and you start to interact with it, in a balanced way, so that things may remain as they are, and you and the reality are both happy in this positive, non-invasive give-and-take.

3. Change - When the *reaction* takes a further step and enters the domain of *no more*. The effort to react and maintain balance, is too big in comparison with the advantages of remaining in this reality.

Never forget to regularly ask yourself if the place where you are, is the place where you wanted to be.
Keep in touch with your true self and your dreams, so that...
WHAT YOU DO
aligns with
WHAT YOU WISH TO DO.

2.10 USING INTUITION

I have got a large amount of inbuilt intuition, and I am very happy about that fact. It increases when you exercise ways to amplify your perceptions, for example, using the suggestions I give you in this book, including the thirty additional suggestions I have collected in the last subchapter. I assure you, that if you take and follow my life-coaching advice, you will witness an awakening, just like you do when a TV set is tuned in to a High Definition channel.

The problem is that we've learnt (from school, parents, friends, movies, and advertising) to act in response to pre-set rational decisions, based on a pre-packaged configuration of what we should instead experience as new. We have learned not to trust, because it has always been connected with *female - wild - unknown. Feeling things instead of analysing or judging* them, helps anchor our life projects to our subconscious mind.

> *Will, determination & perseverance work in their natural element, when they respond to feelings and intuition.*
> *Tuning your thoughts to follow your intuition brings you closer to human nature, and keeps you connected to your true basic needs;*

Those needs are not those created by the industrial revolution!

What we get from this, is a total alignment of our deepest, even hidden inner wishes, to the reality that we build. The process:

Intuition → Thought → Action → Results

The people who allow themselves the application of generative forces such as intuition — besides being true to their own selves — are more likely to accomplish their life's original purpose/s.
That is the realization of a life well-lived
A happy and fulfilled life!

2.11 BEING AUTHENTIC... BEING YOU

Always! Just keep in mind that this may offend other people's sensitivities; it happens when your ego is particularly original, or direct, or excessively brilliant and powerful. It would be just great if you could be authentic, without being rude, too.

Being yourself means leaving space for improvement and development, and being proud of what you are, right now. Self-esteem is the basis for self-confidence. Self-confidence is the basis for any results you want to attain.

The most restricting thing that can happen to your ego/self is subjugating to *other people's* idea of you. Whatever you do, people will form their own opinions, based on micro-variables which you have underestimated or are not in a capacity to control (I will talk more about this later on). So, don't even try! Meet your own objectives, your own tastes.

Dream your own dreams.
Change for your own sake.

This is good advice, and this is what works both in the short and long run, and allows you to be happy!

Nothing is so liberating and happiness-inducing, than the feeling of being true to yourself.

At work, within your family, among your friends: Do not be ashamed of your originality, or your peculiarities.
They are great.
They are YOU!

I have an exercise in the coaching section for YOU.

2.12 REDUCING COMPETION

I am at risk of becoming unpopular, for suggesting something, which totally goes against the flow, but I love my readers much more than sticking to populist theories.

Since the early 80's and the Yuppie generation, the problem of competition, which is as old as Cain, has become more evident… a real plague in fact! Why? Because life-rhythms have changed, and besides coping with the usual compelling tasks, we additionally charge our life with this nonsensical: *"Look… I am better than you!"* theory. I have always thought big, and extended my arms until it hurts, in order to reach the highest and sweetest fruits on the life tree. But I did it uniquely for myself and, later, for me and my family.

> *The will to succeed must come from the will to hit the target, not to win over the competition. This allows for more focus and creativity, and prevents nerve-wracking stress.*

Of course, I observe what the others do, I compare methods, I try to invent and refine efficiency and reap the benefits of alternative ways. I understand that many have to see the challenge, to deliver their best. But a challenge is no less challenging and thrilling if you avoid looking at those running at your sides, or behind you, or in front you! On the contrary…

The horse runs faster and with fewer interruptions by having the blinkers on.

Being competitive is also socially unacceptable, if you think how many friendships and family ties suffer and end because of such an emotional charge.

2.13 THE BAD, THE INDIFFERENT AND THE GOOD ROBOT

Surrounding yourself with the right people and having harmonious and nurturing relationships with them, provides for enriching experiences and minimizes the possibility of conflicts.

There are individuals you almost can't avoid having contact with; for example, parents, boss, teachers, ex-husband/wife if divorced with children. But for the others who are, or will, become friends or business/life partners, it's important to make choices at some stage. I give people lots of possibilities for the relationship to work. I let them come close to me, so that I can see them much better than if I build walls and leave us both with the feeling *I have rejected them* from the very beginning. But there comes a time when I must surrender to the evidence that there is no compatibility of interests and objectives, and that any effort on my part is only going to further negatively charge my happiness. This time cannot be delayed indefinitely, not if you want to live a happy and fulfilled life.

Cultivate only good relationships to master the economics of happiness.

John Bosco – popularly known as Don Bosco, an Italian Roman Catholic priest of the Latin Church, educator and writer of the 19th century – when talking about his youth writes: *"All this time I had to use my own initiative to learn how to deal with my companions. I put them in three groups: the good, the indifferent, and the bad. As soon as I spotted the bad ones, I avoided them absolutely and always. The indifferent I associated with only when necessary, but I was always courteous with them. I made friends with the good ones, and then only when I was sure of them."*

As a life-coach, I have to make concepts edible for the subconscious mind, which is faster and more effective than the conscious mind in defending our territory, sounding the alarm and deploying first-line troops. Therefore, I created a visualization exercise with three robots. Warning: do not go around thinking of putting labels on people, judging, assessing and so on. This is not an absolute method, this is a suggestion to simplify and make your relationship life happier by channelling your efforts into people who will pay off.

Be loving, patient, open minded and tolerant to people before excluding them from your life.

VISUALIZATION

Visualize the subject…

(for example: a friend, colleague, sibling, prospective partner, prospective friend)

> *…as a very simple Robot with 9 Buttons (3 x 3 rows) on its chest.*
> *Pressing one button corresponds to one interaction with that person.*

THE BAD ROBOT is BLACK. Whenever you press the buttons, its *FACE GRINS*, and the *ARMS ARE CROSSED*. A pressed button blinks red. This signals that the person is evil, arrogant, selfish, disloyal, judgmental, harsh, rude, vindictive, unfair, and destructive; they generate and fuel conflicts from nothing.

THE INDIFFERENT ROBOT is WHITE. Whenever you press the buttons its *FACE REMAINS NEUTRAL*, and the *ARMS STAY DOWN*. The pressed buttons only blink sporadically, and produce a faint white light which disappears in the blink of an eye. This signals that the person is insensitive, apathetic, detached, indifferent, impassive, unflappable, indifferent, cold, and disinterested. White is a non-colour. In turn, this is a non-person. These subjects are often confused as being ideal partners and friends, since their whiteness inspires you to write your own story about them – like you would on white paper. You will discover, often too late, that the greater your creativity the better this person and your projections.

THE GOOD ROBOT is AZURE. Whenever you press the buttons, its *FACE SMILES,* the *ARMS ARE OPEN AND OUTSTRETCHED TOWARDS YOU.* The pressed buttons blink with bright yellow, intense light. This signals that the person is warm, open, benevolent, sensitive, altruistic, giving, loving, kind, honest, fair, constructive, polite.

Now, you might want to use this visual system regularly, to assess people who are already present in your life, especially on those you would like to come closer to, such as a prospective partner. You need a certain number of contacts and interactions in order to use this visualization exercise properly. Every interaction is the pressing of a button. How does the robot react? What colour is the light?

Why use a robot analogy? Because visualizing the person while thinking about your interactions with him/her, wouldn't allow you to be objective.

Avoid the bad robots.
Keep cordial, short and non-close relationships
with the white robots.

Befriend only azure robots, and preferably,
the best among them!

These last robots assure brilliant and vibrant interactions, where lot of love will be exchanged. You are an endless source of happiness for one another, covering various and multiple forms, such as respect, empathy, responsibility, openness and a willingness to help and be there for others. The warmth coming from azure robots transforms them into human beings, the only ones who deserve to reach your core and drink the sweet juices of your soul. Please remain tolerant and understanding however… because azure robots are still not perfect! It is perhaps their humanity which makes them so special. They also endure bad times, although they don't plague you with their problems constantly. Keep a special eye on them, because they need you as much as you need them, even though you can live perfectly happily without one another. Happy people, in fact, are not inclined to feel the need to socialize or have social contacts every day.

Happy people can enjoy the company of
silence and listen to the music of their heart.

2.14 SIMPLIFYING YOURSELF

Enjoying the sight and company of small children is enlightening and energizing; kindergartens are temples of joy. Children are angels; they dispense positive energies and teach you how simple life can be, asking for and receiving simple pleasures.

Eliminating pomposity and complexities can be hard. I know. But once you learn, you feel lighter, free and happier... like a child! There are hundreds of books on *how to simplify yourself*. But to be frank, it's all about eliminating everything which has no purpose in your life, including procedures, things, habits and relationships.

Here are a few examples of how I gained time for myself and the things I *like* to do. I rarely use my mobile phone. On working days, I check my email once, at maximum twice a day; on holidays, I will check it every three days, or once a week if I am abroad. I reduced make up quantities and the time taken to put it on; I curbed my time under the shower; so that in ten minutes, I am ready to go out and take my child to school. I use many robots at home to help me with chores, and lots of digital robots to help me with my job. I have eliminated writing Christmas cards and sending gifts to people I have never personally met. I have almost given up reading newspapers – the brief articles of news on the internet and TV news channels are okay, and they're all that I need to keep myself informed. I unplugged my answering machine: if I'm not there, and it's important, the person will surely ring back. If not, the reason they were calling has expired. I talk to people as genuinely as I can and because I always tell the truth, I save time, the time which some people use up to adjust their multiple versions of the truth. I decline invites from people I am not interested in forming a closer connection with; the same approach is used for work offers, appearances, interviews and collaborations for which I miss the necessary élan. I stopped hosting so many parties at home. I don't send SMS messages. I only use emails and phone calls when it is strictly necessary. I am not afraid of showing my fragilities and weaknesses, if any. As a general rule, I don't waste time in doing things, I do not find interesting or necessary. I create processes and optimize them both at work and in my private life, so that repeated actions do not need to be rethought, and I have more time available for endeavours which produce creative happiness.

"I am light, big and strong enough to contain any problem that might arise from my much simpler life."

DID YOU KNOW? - Most of the time we are afraid of problems, accidents or complications which never occur and/or, are far smaller than the efforts we invest in order to prevent them. Life runs on a timeline; consuming it with non-important tasks is not efficient in the Economics of Happiness.

3 30 MORE PROVEN WAYS TO INCREASE YOUR 'HAPPINESS INSIDE'

Always learning and doing something new: Learning means to be open and grasp life lessons from everything/everybody you come in contact with. The best way to keep your mind efficient, and be happy with its abilities and performances, is constant stimulation of the brain cells. Learning new skills, subjects, sports, hobbies, positive behaviours, concepts, and the worlds around them. Curiosity doesn't kill the cat. Boredom does!

BE OPEN TO new thoughts, to new people, to new principles, to new ideas, to new experiences. 'NEW' MAKES US GROW!

Taking care of your appearance: A whole chapter is dedicated to appearance in <u>HAPPY DIVORCE</u>. The key words are: *well-groomed* and a *self-confident body posture*!

Letting it be fun and glamorous: Never lose your playfulness. Pamper yourself and do whatever makes you happy on a regular basis, such as going to the theatre, to the dance, or meeting friends at restaurants and spas, etc. Let the child in you take the initiative. Do not be ashamed of behaving in an original, or even ridiculous way. If you feel you want to go out wearing a pair of bright yellow shoes, even if you have thousand subordinates who will be surprised by your wardrobe choice, just do it!

> *What makes us happy always makes sense,*
> *provided it breaks no laws or hearts!*

We are all trapped in impossible working schedules. Reduce your hours at work and gain free time for your own fun and that of your children. Allow glamour and luxury articles to light up your life every now and again. They can be items which become available as special bargains and/or for free. Happiness is an equalizer, it will make everything better in your life, provided you turn it on!

Talking positively: Happy people rarely use negative phrasing.

> *Our mind isn't able to grasp concepts as*
> *easily when we hear them in a negative form.*
> *If you want to be heard, speak simply and*
> *positively.*

If you want to think positive, you have to talk positive, and vice versa.

Filter and eliminate from your jargon, wording such as: "I hate", "I cannot bear", "that's bad", "I have a problem", "the problem is", "how boring", "I don't like it", "that's stupid", "so horrible", "I can't", "I am not able", "I won't do it", "I won't succeed", and so on and so forth.

Also using the word "never" too often, is not a good idea. "Never" is a Possibility Killer, and you want to have endless possibilities, don't you?

Do the job of your dreams: Or implement any change / modification needed to make your current job more appealing to you.

> *Do the things you like to be happier, stronger & more successful. Only by so is hard work replaced by dedication.*

Meditation: There are many forms of meditation… with and without music in background, group meditation, complemented by breathing techniques. One minute or two hours… any time spent practicing meditation is a balm for your soul and a source of happiness.

Staying connected with nature: Wherever you live, coming in touch with a small piece of nature is never a problem. Creating green corners inside your home, with easy to care for plants, helps harmonize air quality and adds freshness and beauty to your environment. Walking in the park, sitting under a tree, breathing oxygen up in the mountains, rolling on the grass, bathing in a lake, taking a Finnish sauna, laying in the sun, looking at the sky, watching and feeding the birds – these are only a few of endless ideas.

The exchange of energies between nature and ourselves, is equal to that between parents and children.
We all come from Mother Nature and the contact with it is reassuring, soothing, and energizing. The practice of loving nature is one of the most fulfilling forms of love available to us.

Be open, tolerant and non-judgmental: Otherwise, nothing new can enter your life, especially love and happiness!

Stop categorizing and labelling!
This is your way to avoid the "UNKNOWN", but brings the risk of avoiding the "NEW"!

My favourite quote ever is contributed by Mother Teresa, however: *"If you judge people, you don't have the time to love them."*

From love comes love. And love is happiness!

Appreciating every moment:

Every attempt to fix eternity is an escape from reality. I will be plaguing my days with moments and minutes. Forever is too far.

Never looking down at the pavement/ground while walking: Always look above ninety degrees. Observe the architecture of the nearby houses and the form of their roofs; the colour of the automobiles parked in the street; the way the woman in turquoise walks her dog. How many people cross the road without looking left or right? Listen to the birds singing in the trees; observe how happy the face of your waiter is at your favourite restaurant; look up to the sky... are there clouds up there? Is the sky blue or would you describe it as azure?

Look... life is happening all around you!

Hugging and kissing: Your children, your parents, your colleagues, your business partner, your neighbours – at any time and for no reason. Being loving has a boomerang effect! I wish from the bottom of my heart, that you will soon be able to hug and kiss your partner for life!

Smiling for no reason: It creates a habit, improves your appearance, and turns you into a warmer and more attractive human being. The benefits will soon be noticed and reflected by other people (children first!), as well as by animals and plants around you.

Smile, wherever and whenever you can!

Counting to ten before reacting to harassment: I have to admit, that my level of tolerance in this respect has never been particularly high. But I have improved lately, and I am happier because of it, because conflicts poison our life.

At times, what we might consider harassment is just the only way another person has to show you what they think or want, perhaps in a particularly arrogant, and perhaps not particularly polite way. Counting to ten helps to assess the gravity of what you've heard, and respond in a less emotional way, AKA… Be polite yourself!

Being gentle: A kind soul is often considered a weak person. In the long run, everybody will appraise you as being a kind person *and* a strong one!

Being respectful: It means considering the knowledge that people have dignity, feelings, plans, and time of their own to manage, and that the interaction with you should leave the status quo *unvaried or improved* – from their point of view! People who are not used to being respectful, usually do not build positive relationships. A happy person cannot renounce respecting people, our planet and its ecosystem.

Being responsible & taking responsibility: Wherever you are, whatever your role, you are in a position to make a difference. Use this power!

> There are those who listen, those who talk,
> and those who do.
> At best you listen, you talk & you do!
> Be an active player in your circle and make
> history!
> Be an initiator!

The more you take responsibility, the bigger the results in any area of your life. *As a responsible person,* you are automatically considered dependable and trustworthy… the sort of qualities human beings need to build solid and harmonious relationships with others. *As a person who takes responsibility,* for other people as well, you are automatically considered a leader in your community.

Being moderate: The need to prevent excesses; think of food, sports, drugs, or whatever else comes to mind.

> *DID YOU KNOW? - drinking too much water can be lethal (more than five litres for adults, and children can die with only two litres), because it can badly affect the kidneys:*

Sex and moderation? Um… stay away from prospective partners who show no interest for sex. It they are so *cold* at the beginning, they will only be colder later on, excluding rare exceptions.

The concept of moderation is old and it has always been the main preoccupation of religious leaders. Mohammed wrote in the Koran not to drink alcohol or to eat pork, as his people overindulged in their consumption; a social problem because – under the Middle East's hotter temperatures – spirits and heavy foods affect health and behaviour gets worse.

Moderation is a life rule to be infringed upon every now and then, so don't even bother to be absolutely perfect in this regard.

*Exceptions are not only allowed, but required
in order to enjoy life!*

Being Human: I am in favour of sustainable self-development, respecting the person as a *human being*. I am against indoctrination. I am sceptical and condemn any manipulative school of thought or movement asserting that they want to free your self; they often do the opposite instead, by *abusing* your core.

*There are elements in our character, traits
which are not the product of external
influences and make us so special, so unique.
They are our scent and whenever we try to
change our scent, the outcome can be
something other than perfume.*

We are born flexible and adaptable, because the variety of feelings and emotions we display and absorb is wide. Granting this multiplicity of feelings, both *given and received* is critical in our emotional ecosystem.

*Reducing our response in the hope of not
being touched by negative events, will only*

preclude access to other sources of happiness, as well as many possibilities for further self-development.

It is similar to when you limit your diet to just a couple of different foods, because you think that the others could be harmful; on the contrary, they contain important nutrients, and it's only advisable to limit the intake, not stop eating these foods completely. We can improve ourselves by adopting new positive habits, such as you are doing right now by reading this book, or simply trying to acquire something new every day from our own experiences. In both cases, we remain flesh and soul, not machines programmed to react and feel in a given way.

Every man can be a winner and a loser, in the very same day.
Every man can be sad, or very happy, in the very same day.
Every man can be a planet or a brilliant star, in the very same day.

Parents, friends, children, bosses, competitors, enemies (if any!) – are human. Decrease the gap between your fears, expectations and reality! Your partner will also be a human being, even if you order him or her over the internet and under their description you read that they are SUPER MAN or WONDER WOMAN.

Release of control, and feeling compassion for yourself: Those times when you are not perfect, when you are not able to work as efficiently as you are used to doing, or when being single with children seems to be a heavier burden than ever. You may be right! There are, in fact, times when we are required to over-perform and push ourselves to the limit. Just try to do your best. Nobody is perfect and you cannot always be in control of everything. Take your time to relax and regain strength!

Asking for help: When needed! Personally, I have a lot of difficulties with this myself. But I am learning and I have such good feedback, that I'm encouraged to ask for more help!

Less Daily News: An excess of information about what happens around the world, especially when it's very dramatic, can leave a negative impression over your entire day. I have once read of a ten-year-old girl, raped and murdered in Australia. I saw a picture of her on Facebook, and a black curtain dropped over me. A few days later, while driving, I heard on the radio that the corpse of a twelve-year-old girl was found abused and lifeless *on my side of the river*, just five miles south of my home. I started crying, for both her and her family. I also have a daughter! What have I added to my day, besides terror, concern and sadness? What did I do to help the families of these two angels? Nothing! Learning what happened helped no one, except it caused the happiness to disappear from my face for a while. That's it! The same goes for being the carrier of that news. Please avoid *continuously* posting news and images of that kind in your social networks. You do a big favour to yourself and to others by doing so.

Self-Expression through Arts and Exercise: It may be music, painting, dancing, martial arts… whatever requires creativity, sensitivity, focus, attention, discipline and sustains the expression of your core personality.

Being thankful for whatever you have, see, listen to, or touch and it enters your life: Be it in your physical, mental or emotional sphere.

Taking care of your health: Especially through prevention and a life well lived. As few chemicals as possible should enter your home, in any form, from building materials to household products.

Let no one steal your freedom: "We are angels with only one wing, and we can only fly by embracing one another." - Luciano De Crescenzo, Author and Singer.

This is true to a certain extent, because sometimes *the other* can lead the flight. It becomes apparent only when we realize, that the spot where we've landed wasn't on our map. Pay attention!

Painting the world with your favourite colour/s: From clothes, to home furniture, to the things which surround us every day. Add comfort, colour and light to your workplace.

Avoid and/or end conflict-generating relationships: Sometimes it's no one's fault! It lays not in the people themselves, but in their particular personality combination. If you have said and done everything in your power, including using some exotic tricks and generated not even one positive effect, the only way to boost your happiness is lifting your finger and pressing the *OFF switch.*

There are people who leave us with a feeling of uneasiness every time we have contact with them. If we are not meant for each other, we simply have to accept it and let them go!

Going after what you want most: Provided you don't break the law or other people's hearts, everything is allowed!

Changing a decision: Commitment is one of my favourite words. But a commitment can be based on false or insufficient preambles and a poor assessment of a person, project or situation. The many variables contributing to forming a decision, including time, might cause a certain uneasiness with a decision, at a certain point.

71

If you are not comfortable with a decision,
chances are high that it's not the right one
for you.
If you can still change it, do it!

To end this long list with a pearl of wisdom… here is my personal *Happiness Paradigm*, which allows me to overcome any obstacle, to preserve a positive state of mind and to live new and enriching experiences in the physical and emotional realms:

LOVE, EXPLORE, APPRECIATE!

4 RECOGNIZING LOVE WHEN IT APPEARS AT YOUR DOOR

There is something I really cannot bear, and it's the waste of love, in all its forms. It is those instances when we feel love and don't show it, or when we're offered love but are too distracted to acknowledge and value it. Every day in the world, huge quantities of *undelivered* or *returned* love replenish a depot: The *Love Cloud*.

The love you feed to your job, your car, and your hobbies, and the love you feed to other people is a product.

I know, it's a feeling, first and foremost, but indeed it is also a *consumer product*.

True love is not available to buy, however.
True love can sometimes be earned, if you are a good boy or girl.
For most of us it comes and touches us unexpectedly, or it's already there in us, for us and for our beloved ones and it must be externalized.

73

Allegedly, love energizes water, and since we are made of over sixty percent water, guess what the consequences are, when love is lacking in our lives? Experiments have shown changes in the physical qualities of water when people were asked to direct a feeling of *love and thankfulness* towards a sealed glass of water, and a feeling of *denial and hatred* to a second one not far from the first. The water *infused* with *love* produced wonderful, perfect ice crystals, while the water *infused* with *hatred,* showed defects in the building of ice crystals, resulting in an irregular form and number. So, it's untouchable, because love is a form of energy, such as electricity, television and radio broadcasting waves. Love is also quantifiable... we receive the electricity bill and we read it to discover how much of it we've consumed. Unfortunately, an instrument which is able to measure love hasn't yet been invented. In essence, if we receive a basket of fresh fruit as a gift, we see the fruit, and we eat it.

The invisibility of love, it's essence as energy, requires special effort, and for us to paint it with externalizations.

Imagine love as a transparent dummy, whose silhouette takes form only by covering it with words, hugs, kisses, assistance, smiles, shared

time, sex, and whatever else comes to your
mind.
Every piece of externalization is a piece more
of love being revealed!
If you love, show your love!

On the other hand, it's curious that sometimes we search for love, but when it comes to visit us, reveals itself in all its brilliant and vibrant colours… we still don't see it, or we don't grasp that it is the right one, or the best chance in our lives to be happy. It can be a new job we're offered and we're too lazy to evaluate; or the offer of help from someone we do not deem capable of helping us; or the love of a special person, whom we don't see as special, because our heart isn't open or our mind is distracted. Between parents and children, the love exchange can be activated at any age. I started kissing my father on the cheeks at fourteen; we were shy and uneducated in regards to how to reveal our love to each other, but our efforts paved the way towards a lifelong, happy relationship.

The love we give and the love we take are both products. Remember it, and remember that a product must be put on show, on the shelves, for people to see and grasp it!

5 SINGLE PARENT LIFE IS NOT NECESSARILY THAT BAD

I am an avowed single. Not because I particularly like to be alone, but because there are only a few things I cannot do without a man. Thus, having a partner is a choice of the heart, not a need.

5.1 "POOR ME! PARENTING 'X' CHILDREN PRETTY MUCH ALONE. IF ONLY I COULD FIND A PARTNER TO SHARE MY PREOCCUPATIONS AND THE RESPONSIBILITIES!"

As a divorced mom, with a ten-year-old girl at home, I have favoured distant but regular contacts with my ex-husband, in order for him to undertake his responsibilities as the father of our child, but also because of the presence of unresolved conflicts between us. What really created a more peaceful exchange of information regarding our child, and only about our child – and for the child's sake only – was the CHILDRENS LOGBOOK (unfortunately only for a short time, then my ex started to ignore it).

The logbook follows the children back and forth from parent-to-parent.

I bought one with a key (one for me and one for my ex-husband), so that my child could not look inside as it's being transported in her luggage from one home to the other. There was pertinent information regarding the child, and eventually, instructions for the other parent to remember, such as special dates, lessons, appointments for the child, etc. The logbook is a communication tool, which makes it easy for both parents to inform and ask each other about holiday programs, for example. The logbook is a neutral messenger and no-one can complain about the information conveyed through it. Okay, if you want, you can *speak* with your ex, of course. But if your relationship suffers from chronic communication problems, the written word is the best, as it allows you to consider whether or not what you are writing is really in the interest of the child or is just a petty request. *Verba volant, scripta manent!* (Latin for *Spoken words fly away, written words remain.*) I used the logbook, for example, to inform my ex in writing about special health issues at delivery: *"Please take particular care this weekend... Camilla is very tired and coughed a couple of times. AKA no stress."* Or *"The piano lesson will end later next Wednesday. So, please remember this when you pick her up from school."* In the logbook, I always inserted copies of school correspondence, notes, and remarks, so that my ex could never complain he was not being informed about Camilla's learning and development.

I promote the exchange and sharing of information and responsibilities as parents between my ex and myself, despite our strong personal differences.

If it's not me who starts positive changes, I cannot expect the other party to do the same.

Let it go, and use the time when your children are with their dad/mom to finally do something for yourself, such as gardening, wellness activities, parachuting, going to a dance, dating etc. Let your mind be free of preoccupations. Keep an eye on what your ex and your children do every now and then, by all means; their control of hygiene, what sort of foods they're eating, where they are travelling to, if it is of a longer distance. But don't interfere with their habits and plans unless they are objectively risky and they threaten the physical and psychological wellbeing and safety of the children. Fathers tend to take more risks than mothers when they spend time with their children. For instance, I learnt to drive at the age of eight with my father.

This is their time together, and apart from a couple of hints now and then, if needed, it's good that the children become confident with a different outlook on life than yours. You cannot provide them with all the love and incentives they require. The more people they have to feed their emotional hunger, curiosity and learning needs, the more rounded they will be as future adult individuals. The other parent provides new substance for their growth and development, hopefully.

You also need more time for yourself and for your new partner… when it comes to you finding one. Precious time needed to get to know each other, without the children creating premature bonds with a person who is not necessarily going to become your partner for life. If you are not widowed, or there are no serious reasons (such as imprisonment or mental disabilities) to hinder contact with the other parent, wherever they happen to be on the Earth, then they should be enabled to provide your children with extra experiences and love.

Even at costs of having to bear conflicts through the contact with the other parent, allow yourself to be helped and relieved while packing your children's Suitcase for Life.

Should you lose contact with your ex, I would advise you to look for a fresh new start with *co-parenting* if and when contact is re-established. Only an abusive ex should be kept far away from your children.

Of course, having a man and a woman at home, helps the children to build more awareness of their gender roles. There are typical things which boys usually do with their dads, and girls with their moms, which can possibly be done by either genders. But I understand that it's not the same, and that the parents who are left alone to cover another gender role, can nurture deep feelings of inadequacy. Many single dads and moms are urged to find a partner, because they feel they have to provide the right emotional support to their children. But, meanwhile...

In order to avoid making rushed and unsatisfying choices involving a future partner, any female and male individuals close to your family and home, be they relatives, friends or civil servants, can successfully provide valid role-leading support to your children.

Ask for cooperation – for example; if your brother can take your boy canoe fishing, should you be a female reader… or, if you are a single dad, ask your fantastic neighbour, a mother of three, if she can escort your daughter to shop for her first tampons and pads.

5.2 "I DON'T EVEN REMEMBER THE LAST TIME I HAD SEX. I THINK MY SEXUAL ATTRIBUTES NEED A CHECK TO SEE IF THEY STILL WORK PROPERLY!"

As a matter of fact, I managed to live without sex for a length of time which I previously never thought to be possible. I am a sensual woman, and sex with my partner is very important to me… a sanctuary of melting into one another and experiencing pure lust. Notwithstanding the above, I discovered that…

Craving for sex is not a permanent condition. After practicing sexual abstinence for some time, the body naturally enters sexual hibernation!

If you want to prevent it from happening, you can have casual sex. Personally, I don't feel compelled to do it. You can practice abstinence and switch on *stand-by* until the right moment comes, without *desperately searching* for someone.

I grant you that your sexual attributes will work as they always have, the next time you have sex. They won't rust, even when we talk about several years of abstinence!

So, never have this preoccupation and keep calm!

If you are looking for casual sex, be wary of your choices and take responsibility for any eventual fall out: they might end up wanting more than a one-night stand!

Happiness has a lot to do with simplicity and respect of natural life cycles!

If the separation from your ex is still a bleeding wound, you might not yet be prepared to sustain the ups and downs, as well as the risks of exposing yourself to new acquaintances. Cave animals normally go into seclusion until their wounds are healed.

Sometimes it is preferable to let your body and soul sleep and heal, rather than awakening your senses for something which may eventually result in more heartache.

Take a deep look into yourself and be true to yourself, before going out for an all-you-can-eat experience. Reply to the following question whenever you come to a pivotal moment in your encounter:

"What do I want to get from this?"

The answers should be *LOVE* or *SEX*. It is simple! Imagine *LOVE* and *SEX* as blinking lights on the head of the person in front of you. Which one is green?

I'm joking! I just wanted to focus your attention on responsible sex. Please, focus your interest on the person you're dating, not on blinking signals over their heads! We get more information about a new acquaintance through our subconscious than our conscious mind. This is the reason why, at times, you know the right answers to your questions, but you cannot put them into words, or you can do it only following deductive reasoning. Trust the first instinct, not regarding the outer shell, but about the personality and relational factors.

Appearance is a relative factor, which can change from repulsive → to neutral → to cute, as soon as certain circumstances, such as sharing experiences-principles-feelings-beliefs-hobbies, enter your romantic scenery. Your animal instinct senses a prospective partner!

For me it's particularly important to establish a connection via my basic instincts... odours, perfumes, a light in the eyes which betrays desire, or a change in the voice modulation, particular movements or poses, and a lot more – all affect and arouse sexual and emotional responses.

Consider that all the stories about werewolves might have a basis in truth. Certain innate, but normally unused, abilities and powers are triggered by fear, pain, love, joy, hate, and danger. This also happens when nature is at work for helping multiplication and renovation, AKA birth and death.

Our animal part – the subconscious – starts computing the information it collects – the same as a radar – when your body enters the other body's energy field. Inside this invisible room, everything can happen through the vibration and resonance of your cells: Body Talk!

Your body and that of your date/encounter, separated from their conscious identities - which are the product of education, cultural and social background, TV adverts and so on – communicate about sex, while in parallel, you are talking about your new career as a blogger, or about how nasty your neighbour's dog is. This first, raw – still not re-modelled information – is the most precious relationship substance, because as time goes by, your conscious mind filters all this substance through its own perceptions, which are sometimes not aligned with your true personal goals concerning a new partner.

Think of your past relationships and the first impression you've got about your partners.

I can only confirm that the first impression, which might have changed later on, was the right one – both about the person and the relationship aspects connected to them. Again, we have been provided with sensors by nature, aimed at obtaining selected reproduction. So, we have to trust these sensors. I first met my ex-husband at a carnival party; he was dressed as a baby (including a huge pacifier in the middle of his face) and wearing shorts, while I was a 70s ere diva, wearing a long cocktail dress. We had a conversation regarding South America and a motor company we both worked for, on different continents. We danced so wildly that I lost a heel and my dress ripped under the left armpit. He was twenty-six, and I was thirty. I discovered that talking with him was exceptionally pleasant, but his baby face was merely the mirror of his immaturity. I resolved there and then, that I was not at all interested in meeting up with him again except on a pure, intellectual basis.

When he first phoned my home, two days later, I decided I didn't want to see him again at all; so I pretended that it was my sister who was answering the phone, and that I was out of town, in the mountains. It was the first and last time I have ever lied to someone over the phone! It was an unexpected decision on the part of my sub-conscious, as soon as I heard his voice on the line. There was such a maturity gap between us, I felt no desire to go strolling downtown and have an ice cream with him. I asked myself why I'd given him my telephone number in the first place, and considered it a mistake I would never make again. In fact, it was the biggest mistake of my life! He phoned again three months later, when he travelled back through my town. He was a young German student, passing his last exam. I was the general manager of a small, international consulting company. He convinced me to go to the beach with him, and when he saw my butt being kissed by the sun, he said to himself *"I want it!"* (He used to tell me this story repeatedly, as a joke. I'm just repeating it.) As most intelligent women on this Earth nonsensically do, I capitulated before his adoration. The End is known, especially to the readers of <u>Happy Divorce!</u>

You are likely to be able to recall my story, more than the principle behind it, because a story can take roots in different areas of your brain.

With each new encounter, you may want to stop and listen to your *feelings*.

Chances are good, when starting from neutral feelings. When your feelings towards someone are negative from the very beginning, you should trust that everything you attempt and invest time into, will be put to the test, and possibly fail to deliver the wished results.

OPPORTUNITY = from neutral to exciting feeling

DANGER = a negative feeling at first look.

Should you receive no signals from your inner feelings, don't force the situation. Maybe this neutrality is an opportunity, or perhaps it's just a lack of any real interest!

5.3 "As soon as I find Mr. / Ms. Right, I'm going to travel to Japan."

This is a parody of everything you leave undone, while hoping and waiting to do it together with your future partner. *I still have to visit Japan!*

I had been with my ex-husband for about sixteen years, and besides *not* travelling to Japan, I also gave up going on ski holidays, and doing a lot of other interesting things which had formerly made my life glamorous, happy and exciting.

Whatever is in your heart, let it be now.
Don't wait for another person to fulfil your wishes, if you are in a position to fulfil them yourself.
Your happiness is your responsibility!

6 FINDING AND BECOMING THE RIGHT LOVING PARTNER

In the effort to provide inspiration and guidance, I won't make a point of being complete and exhaustive about any subject in particular, because every chapter and/or subchapter alone is worth reading an entire book. By way of exemplification, I just divide loving partners into three Groups: The Virus, The Butterfly and The Perfect Partner.

6.1 First Group: THE VIRUS

"Now that I am with X, I can finally focus on myself!"

They would never admit it openly, not even to themselves, but a conspicuous part of the world population is looking – in disorderly, chaotic, random motion – for a partner for life. They come to rest when the body of a *Love Mate* is infected and a long-term/marriage commitment is agreed upon. They've crossed the final line. This is the reason why managers view wedding rings with a benevolent eye, and subliminally encourage employees to get married, because these people can finally transfer into their jobs, the efficiency, energy and mental focus previously used for seeking a love partner! Being in a long term relationship or a marriage is so reassuring, that it inspires some people to explore new ways of self-expression, new hobbies, and sometimes indulge in a bunch of new sporting activities, either alone or with friends.

6.2 SECOND GROUP: THE BUTTERFLY

On the other hand, there is a portion of the world population able to achieve important goals and run a fulfilling life as a single person, because they can use the whole portfolio of their energies for their own personal purposes. What comes in any package with long-term commitments is indeed time & energy-consuming: children, augmented household chores, activities with the partner and the family of the partner, etc. The Butterfly is aware of the responsibilities connected with a partnership, and sometimes they purposely don't become involved, in order not to reduce their freedom, the glow of a brilliant career, and unlimited time for their personal interests. When they enter a love relationship, though, they usually take it seriously and are completely immersed in the role of dream man/woman, perhaps for years… until the single instinct awakes - for example, a new career challenge, wearisome exclusiveness, or high-performing husband / wife / parent role modelling.

Now, while the First Group with Virus-like characteristics acquires Butterfly-like attributes only as part of a couple, the Second Group can be a happy – not absolutely happy – but a happy Butterfly as a single person.

> *Have you noticed something important while reading? Yes, it's the Focus on Oneself!*

*You can only become a beautiful Butterfly
when you don't lose track of your own
wishes-dreams-life projects and you allow
room for further personal development!*

This is very important to keep in mind, both for yourself and for your prospective partner, whose personal space should be recognized and preserved, with your help! I have seen too many couples coming to the brink of divorce and then postponing it, until it has really become too much of a drama. The relationship becomes like black tar for the soul and the body (in the form of depression and psychosomatic illnesses) – therefore creating psychological evil consequences by living in an unhappy relationship and life.

Compromising between personal and family goals is not easy. Responsible parents do compromise over jobs, social networks and personal calls, in order to create harmony, wellbeing, and care for the welfare of their family. But responsible parents must never forget to maintain a healthy balance between the resources invested in the family, and those which have to be reserved and used to be genuinely happy for themselves. With this purpose in mind, I designed EXERCISE 3 – HAPPY PARENTING.

Now, you may argue that there is another aspect to consider in the Virus Group: those looking for a partner and not feeling content until they have found one, but are then revealed to be less present and less active as caregivers than the Butterflies. They take less responsibility in parent role sharing. Yes, the man or the woman who seems to have stepped out of a romantic bestseller novel, using poetic words and imageries as well as a number of other seducing strategies, is indeed the one who proves to be more egocentric as a partner, as soon as they have settled into the relationship. This observation can be useful to take responsibility and to be aware of the following…

> The goal of a loving partnership is to be happy 'with' the partner and 'beside the partner', not 'aside the partner'.

You can see a moral sense in that, as do I. But I also see it as the only way to be happy in the long term, within a loving relationship and the family dynamic.

6.3 Third Group: THE PERFECT PARTNER

I play with the word *perfect*, since perfection is not an absolute concept. Apart from setting forth some of his/her major characteristics…

> *The Perfect Partner exists only in the heart and the mind of the person who loves him/her.*

This is why I limit myself to the spiritual world, to the basic qualities, those making any relationship a happy and fulfilling one. Any other aspect is so subjective, and dependent on your own personal tastes and wishes, that nobody should be allowed to say a word about them.

And now, let me talk about a simple principle: balancing give-and-take. Any organism, any machine, anything which works, and that is living/existing *to perform*, needs to be fed with energies and/or fuel.

> *In the organism 'couple' there are two external agents which are responsible for the continuation of life in this third organism. In our western civilization, the concept of one*

95

partner sustaining this organism alone, be it the husband or the wife, doesn't work.

This is why many attempts to save deteriorating or consumed relationships (those lacking fuel), which have been long sustained and nourished by only one of the agents, fail miserably.

Now, if I withdraw more money than I deposited from my bank account, at a certain point in time I will receive a call from a nice bank official, who will politely say: *"We are so sorry for bothering you, but we noticed that you have overdrawn your account. We would be so very grateful if you could balance your account."*

Do you need a call, to understand when there is something out of balance in your relationship?

No man or woman is particularly eager to see their partner going out alone with their friends, or dedicating more than a couple of hours a week to their own physical and mental circuits! But you also need this freedom, fresh air, energy supply and exchange. Conversely, you must grant them to the partner you love.

On the other hand, leaving the partner at home, while you work on any sort of exciting new life experiences predominantly with your friends, carries the consequence that one day you will find no-one waiting for you at home when you come back. And it will happen, sooner or later – whether it's the 20th or the 1024th time – you will eventually come back home to find yourself alone!

In essence: in the Third Group there are intelligent perfect partners and parents, who are able to supply fuel to their love & partnership, to be responsible in their parenting role, and to look at life as a whole group of possibilities to be discovered together as a couple, as a family, but also alone. Is it difficult? It is an art form! And you can put into it, as much creativity as you want, enjoying the ride with gusto!

> *Perfect partners and parents will glow with such a bright, charismatic aura – that for singles and non-singles passing by, they will be hard to resist!*

Let's now discover the main characteristics which the perfect partner embodies and externalizes:-

Integrity (Honesty+Truthfulness), Responsibility & Respect: This is the magical combination, transforming any frog into a fairy tale prince. Our society needs these sort of people… in fact, is hungry for these sort of people, because society is only half good!

Openness, Sensitivity and Empathy: No partner should build walls. Reciprocal respect will provide the ability for everybody to preserve their own privacy, without the need to set specific boundaries. Openness and sensitivity should include the availability to listen and be empathic. Admitting to being wrong and saying *"I'm sorry"* is also part of the game. As stated before, in the list of hints to be happier; presenting yourself with your vulnerabilities visible helps others to open themselves to you. When walls and fences set limits to self-expression within a couple, intimacy will be of low quality, or totally absent.

The perfect partner exudes so much sentimental stability and spiritual density that you can almost touch them.

Sexual Response and Affection: Showing interest in your partner and being affectionate – hugging, kissing, caressing, alluring and be inviting. You can read a book together and stay completely silent for a couple of hours, and then draw closer to one another and give yourselves a nice hot break, with a coffee (the coffee being the second hot thing in the break) and something sweet at the end. You can return to your reading, after your sexual break, if you want. It need not be planned or for a particularly special reason. It must be regular! The perfect partner is always proud to show their partner how sexy they are, and how their desire is not reducing with time. Sexual intimacy is a connection with our animal part. We can stay friends with our partner, and bear years without sex, but the longer the time since the last body contact, the bigger the distance between those two souls.

Trust: The perfect partner is a trustworthy person, who trusts their partner in turn. I see long-lasting relationships where trust is lacking from one or both sides… they are hell! I have to be able to trust my partner for life, or I might as well quit! Trust makes communication really solid and avoids so many questions about *where* and *with whom* the other is spending their time! Trust is something I try to teach to my daughter, too.

> *There is no light in a relationship, whatever its nature, without trust.*

Sense of Humour: I know most problems between my parents reside in the fact that my father is light-hearted and my mom very serious. The first tells jokes; the second reports the daily news, including the exact death toll for car accidents over the last weekend. A sense of humour means taking life and your partner as lightly as possible.

> *The perfect partner is not obsessed with a single word their beloved one has said in a conversation, or a single episode of behaviour. The perfect partner also knows that there is*

a time to laugh and a time to be serious,

and there are also times to be both...

because life is too short to quarrel over

unimportant things.

I've learned to be light-hearted relatively late in life, as I was a very serious child and teenager. If I can do it, everybody can! I enjoy being the one who adds smiles to a conversation, and I expect my partner to be as light-hearted as I am.

Commitment to good Communication: Polluted communication should not exist. I mean, the situations where partners hide their feelings, regarding both their partner and their own professional or social background.

The perfect partner should try to dedicate an

exclusive channel to their partner, where no

others have the power to interfere.

That may seem a far too idealistic concept, but love creates wonders, and when you love your partner, and you talk with him/her, you should be able to listen and talk to him or her alone. *The Others* should be and remain, distanced during these conversations. Interferences of any kind are guilty of provoking more than a distraction in beautiful relationships. Therefore, pay attention to your attitude. Are you conveying too many feelings which do not belong in the conversation? Stop yourself and resume the conversation once you are in a mood to be nice to your partner. Stress, headaches & other situations are understandable, but conversations containing only a few syllables, or ones which don't include questions regarding your partner, are *not* conversations… they are, in fact, mumblings and monologues to be exercised, preferably alone, under the shower. Understanding if and when there are communication problems and committing to improving them is essential. Without making the partner feel as if he/she is talking nonsense, *the perfect partner will work to ensure communication keeps flowing and remains interesting for both parties.*

A couple goes through a number of critical moments and ages in a lifetime: sickness and death of dear ones, financial restraints and psychological ups and downs.
In this landscape you should see a sunny spot… that is you as a couple, and what you have built together!

My book is meant to both spot them and to teach you how to be a Happy Perfect Partner!

First and foremost... start to be true!
Whatever it costs, whatever happens. Stay
true.

The word *True* has almost as much positive resonance as the word *Love*. Just talking about love for a couple of hours takes people to higher levels of perception and understanding! Senses work 150 times better: for example, you can hear more low-level sounds, and smell perfumes, which might have previously remained undetected.

Love in a poem makes it good.
Love in a conversation makes it better.
Love in your life makes miracles!
Let Love enter your body and your soul and
start your awakening, to acceptance of the
beauty of a new partner in your heart.

Love happens, and you might fall in love at first sight for a number of reasons – which have nothing to do with true love, rationality and self-development. It is known that not all kinds of love turn into a relationship, or at least, a long-term one – if some criteria are not satisfied, especially those I have listed above. And because you search for advice and inspiration in my book, you are among those people who want to build relationships and not stay idle and alone their whole life.

The charismatic personality of the perfect partner, the pillar of a balanced, caring and exciting relationship, is a treasure to be shown, especially to prospective partners. Displaying your points of view is akin to exposing your goods in a marketplace; if you keep them under the counter, nobody will buy them.

When you learn to do this, you will receive positive feedbacks from those sharing your vision. If you are a man, and you don't feel at ease talking about how you feel regarding a long-lasting relationship, you might want to practice with a close friend or a coach (like me) and learn how to do so. When you make your beautiful personality transparent to the opposite gender, you get an excellent emotional return on your investment. Don't forget to... *Focus on yourself, your wishes, your life projects. Maintain and keep room for further personal development.*

7 ONLINE DATING? IF YES, THEN... GO AND SHINE!

We all end up using online dating services, at least once in our life. After a divorce or a break up from a long relationship, it becomes almost routine: the art of appealing, for the sake of attracting a partner into our life has become as abstract as one of Kandinsky's paintings. Moreover, there never seems to be enough time, especially in the midst of big divorce-generated changes, to just go out and make casual acquaintances.

Open you heart to Love: love Love and the feeling of being loved in a sensual, sexual and spiritual way.

Most marriages ending with divorce lacked at least two of the three above components. You might need to awaken body & soul while preparing for a great new age of love conquests. This is the time to improve and polish your appearance, if needed. In essence:

First enjoy playing, then enter the game!

This new, regenerating, exciting feeling of love expectation also helps us to cope with the uneven ground of the newly acquired 'single' status. You decide – not your parents, not your friends, not your children, or whoever else – what you want next in your life!

Love can be short-, long-lasting, intermittent, serious, blasphemous, weird, flirtatious, binding, free, and so on. You must feel at ease and aligned with your wishes, in order to be happy and successful in your quest for love. Be true to yourself and prospective partners. If you want to flirt, don't make any promises. An ethical attitude always offers a return! If you want the big fish, you must use big bait. No short cuts, no discounts, and no tricks.

Description: Appearance, Age, etc.: You've registered on a dating website, and you're required to enter your initial data regarding yourself.

There really is no point in claiming to be forty years old, when you are twenty years older. The same rule applies to your physical attributes.

Apart from creating poor after-date opportunities (waiting for Brad Pitt and having dinner with Danny DeVito instead… is BAD!), the risk of being banned from the site you have selected is high.

> *DID YOU KNOW? - There are hundreds, if not thousands of niche-market dating websites, designed and targeted to specific clientele. You can find them by Googling: +singles +website +dating + 'your special trait/wish'.*

Using this theory, I found, for example, websites targeting single parents, overweight singles; specializing in older people seeking a younger partner and one for every height.

Income: There are only a few websites where you are required to insert a value, otherwise in the majority of cases you are free to leave the question blank, whether you're listed in Forbes World's Billionaires or not!

By-line: This is the phrase, or a couple of lines which you are required to add to your picture, to garner the attention of your 'fish'.

> *Never leave the by-line blank!* Gain the advantage by telling your prospective 'fish' something intriguing but honest. This is your promo!

It causes beautiful searchers to 'CLICK' and check out your profile, instead of scanning past you. *Think of your best qualities as a person, as one half of a couple, and as a parent if applicable.* Describe what you are good at. Ask your closest friends what they like best about you. They might highlight interesting characteristics, which you have previously ignored! *Ponder on each word.* Competition is *huge* out there. Be concise. Possibly use the Twitter style 'adjective + substantive' instead of whole sentences, for example:

'*I very much like cooking for family and friends*' becomes: 'Great social cook'

'*I am good at observing the rhythms of nature and responding accordingly, so that my garden, my job and my family life are harmoniously run by universal laws*' becomes: "Spiritual nature-lover".

Finally... Reserve a couple of words for what you look for in a partner, and filter out unwanted contacts.

About you - Profile: This is the longer description, usually requested after the first round of general data collection and should follow the same rule: *short, appealing and honest.* It is advisable to include eventual chronic diseases and/or other critical information, which might heavily affect the lifestyle or life quality of your future partner. For example, diabetes or being the parent of eight children living with you, or having an overnight job. Ideally, you should write your profile in the form of a short story, containing:

- 10% your past

- 10% your work
- 20% your interests, hobbies
- 10% ideals and life projects
- 20% what you offer to a partner
- 20% what you want to do with your dream partner and,

Last but not least…

- 10% description of your ideal partner.

Organizing your Profile/Long Description as a story means 50% more possibilities to be remembered, that is literally standing out from the masses. Therefore, NO LISTS but A STORY! You can ask for or pay for help if you are not a natural-born writer.

DID YOU KNOW? - There are a number of dating-profile editors online. Try to find one by Googling: +dating +profile +editing.

Profile Picture: A large percentage of men's profile pictures, discourage any woman's attempts to acquire new acquaintances through the internet or apps. I appreciate much more, the effort of those using Photoshop (which women do very often), since *improvement* is the key. The phenomenon is statistically important; because it concerns more than seventy percent of the men's pictures, which I've seen around dating websites, including those with expensive membership costs. Women are used to thinking in terms of *appearance*, while men have grown up focusing on their inner qualities, such as the power of money, their social competences. Forget it! We women like to see how good looking you are! We would rather choose to click on a profile with a picture of a man smiling nicely, rather than one of a man looking extremely depressed or weird. As far as single parents, separated and divorced people are concerned, they're tired of dealing with problems and are eager to enjoy the frivolous side of life. Every person wants to like their date. I'm sure it seems as if I'm pointing out something extremely obvious. But if you come over to my side of the screen, you'll notice that...

> *...at the base of the problem, there must be some false assumptions and beliefs about what women find interesting or are able and willing to tolerate in a man.*
>
> *For example, it's a false assumption that all women like funny-looking men!*

A GOOD PHOTOGRAPH SHOULD BE YOUR FIRST INVESTMENT ON A DATING WEBSITE...

THE INVESTMENT!

You may want to have a professional photo shoot done, and choose from one to three appealing pictures to catch the eye of your visitors. This is what came out during my personal survey and are things you should avoid. Enjoy!

1. Blurred pictures are romantic.

2. My blurred picture, with me turning my back to the camera, is hilarious.

3. I know for sure that my clown-face makes women want me even more!

4. The toilet in the background is just gorgeous; we must always remember that we are human beings, just a slightly more intelligent species of animal!

5. My children are far more photogenic than their mom/dad. Which is why I let them occupy the whole picture! Moreover, it's now clear that I am a family woman/man, a very engaged mom/dad. My ideal partner must first and foremost be a good mother/father. Love will come later!

6. My white t-shirt is the latest fashion trend worldwide! Okay... so it's no longer so white after 5 days of wear, but it's still an eye-catcher!

7. My closed eyes are just perfect, since prospective partners can imagine them to be any colour they want!

8. I love my pets above all, and my future partner must know it before engaging. And yes, they will of course continue to sleep in my bed… my 2 dogs, my guinea pig and my 2 Siamese cats. All of them!

9. Ungroomed is macho.

10. Oversize outfits turn her/him on.

11. The picture with my ex-husband/wife and I, hugging and kissing, is the proof that I am a great lover and a relationship-oriented person.

12. This in the background is my home and my castle. I am sure that every woman will be eager to make it tidy and buy some pieces of furniture, just as soon as she moves here.

13. Yes, this is my mom; and the one right behind her is me. She is there in all circumstances! But I love her.

14. Women love to wait. They want it slow! I thought that uploading no picture is a sign of understanding a women's deeper nature and expectations. There is always time, later on, to send a picture.

15. Yes… the Ferrari, the yacht, and the villa in Malibu were all mine, but I lost them during my last trip to Las Vegas.

16. I don't see what's the matter with my white, reasonably bald-head and the fact that I've claimed to be forty years of age! I think I am still young at heart at seventy... picture or no picture!

17. I don't often smile, and I thought you should know how sad I am! This is a way to be true to myself and to my future partner! Give me a Kleenex, please!

18. Yes, I am really proud of all my children. There wasn't enough room in the picture for all of us, so I only put the kids in the photo.

19. Yes, my faith is very important to me, and the one-pound, solid gold crucifix hanging over my naked, hairy chest in my photo makes it clear who comes first.

20. Oh, sorry... that's Jenny, my personal assistant. She went to the photo shoot at my place, while I was chairing a stakeholders meeting! But you can trust her one hundred percent. I will personally put my signature on all of the emails she sends you on my behalf.

21. Hey...don't make a drama out of it, girl! My old black-and-white Polaroid displays a wonderful baby smile! Women are known to have a great imagination. They should have the opportunity to use it every once in a while!

22. Sunglasses are absolutely a must in a portrait picture. They convey a dramatic look, which intensifies a person's

experience and perception while visiting my profile. Everybody should wear sunglasses on their dating-profile pictures!

23. No, this isn't me or my dad in the picture. Of course! Yesterday was the tenth anniversary of my granddad's death; so this picture is in his memory. Anyway, do you have anything against dating a much older guy?

24. Please, don't be so selective, difficult and intolerant about pictures! I just picked the first I found on Men's Health/Cosmopolitan. So what? He/She looks very much like I do, apart from the body.

25. I never-never-never put pictures online or send them via e-mail. You never-never-never know what people will use them for! For example, photomontages showing me in a pornographic pose, these sort of things happen all the time, you know! So… no exceptions. My future partner must accept me as I am, entirely for my soul, not for my appearance, anyway!

26. Yeah, I was eating pizza and the white lava coming out of my mouth is simply mozzarella cheese.

27. I just think it's important that a woman/man who's connecting with me is able to learn who I really am from the very first contact. That's why I show up naked in all my pictures. You know exactly what you're *buying*!

28. In the precise moment when I was uploading my picture, hurricane Gina hit my town. That's why you can only see half of the picture. My upper body is forever lost to the hurricane or somewhere on the internet... who knows! But from my hairy legs, I think it's quite clear that you're dealing with first class male stuff!

29. It was a bit dark in my room when I took this picture, I must admit! But in the end, if you put your screen under a light source, you should be able to see my nose.

30. I wish to share with *prospective dates,* the song of my life. That's why I featured the cover of my favourite CD as my profile picture!

31. It's embarrassing, but all I can really tell you, is that it wasn't me who subscribed to this dating site, but my mom on my behalf. After divorcing for the fourth time, she wants me to get married again... ASAP. She thought it would be a good idea to show how much we care for each other by uploading a picture of both of us. No... the bearded guy on the right is my mother; that one on the left, wearing a lycra pink overall, is me!

32. Nature is very important to me. I am a natural creature. I like surrounding myself with natural things. A digital picture is not natural at all. When you put it online, they add strange light effects, and enhance the colours. It just wouldn't be the true me in the picture! I sent a picture of my olive tree instead,

which really embodies all that I am... a solid... green... unmovable... *natural being.* I love nature more than human beings. It's a pity I can't have sex with my olive tree!

33. I love make up; the more the better!

7.1 KEY CONSIDERATIONS TO BE KEPT IN MIND WHILE ONLINE DATING

You start texting because something magic appeared and you feel attracted to this *internet connection*. You have not met each other in the physical world, yet. Despite this, a relationship is already born! There are some things to consider at this point:

1. You have your own *SENSE OF WORTH*, which is the historical result of your experience through:

   a. *people's feedback*

   b. *your own perception of your value*

2. You have your own *SENSE OF ROMANCE*, which is the result of your:

   a. *old wounds*

   b. *wishes*

   c. *needs*

   d. *hopes & expectations.*

3. You have your *SENSE OF REALITY* as a single parent, which is also the sum of situations and challenges generated by:

a. ex-partner/spouse

b. job

c. children

d. time management

e. financial changes

f. social changes

g. emotional sensitivity ← {concerns, setting up of new life rules, too much complexity}

In a normal situation, where two people meet and start going out together, they come face-to-face with their:

$$\textit{Sense of Worth + Sense of Romance + Sense}$$
$$\textit{of Reality} =$$
$$\textit{LOVE PERSONALITY}$$

Now, please go back to the list, and ~~strike out~~ the items which are not touched/modified/challenged by an *online relationship*. You will realize that many of the items are left aside, while your virtual relationship progresses into something with a definite individuality and identity: a *love story between two* 'incomplete' *Love Personalities*. The hindrance comes not only from both being physically unreachable, but also from what we normally use to convey feelings and emotions into the online love relationship. Whether the visual component is included or not - video chat, instead of emails or written messages for example, the medium itself gives both Love Personalities the possibility to show themselves *without noises*. And noises are part of daily life. I am describing acquaintances based on honest and genuine reciprocal interest, excluding love frauds.

In essence, no one is investing material and spiritual assets, status quo, future projects or existing relationships. Only feelings are involved, which can be sprayed on one another in pure form, *without fear of losing anything...*

Many items which form a Love Personality, are not required as a compound in this kind of relationship. It goes without saying, that no online acquaintance or relationship can be trusted and qualified as *real*. Therefore...

Keep the online interaction to a minimum and go into the physical world, ASAP!

That will save you lot of time and disappointment in case you are not really meant to be together. In the last section there are two exercises, one for men, and one for women, which will prepare you to master the first date.

Don't delay in meeting each other in person. If your online acquaintance refuses to meet, it can be a strong sign that they are not interested in a serious relationship.

8 WE MET EACH OTHER... AND NOW WHAT?

I am against strategies and tactics meant to change your core, your original nature. I bring forth the idea of sustainable self-development, which helps, improves, and preserves your own human nature, and doesn't turn you into a different individual. A positive attitude (like those I listed in the *Perfect Partner* subchapter) enriches, gives a plus, doesn't deprive people of their ability to feel and respond with empathy to social interactions. Don't accept schools of thought and coaches who put *control* above anything, because that is as threatening as transforming humans into machines.

You also don't need to enter a competition to be noticed and loved by a *special someone*. Competitions are nerve-wracking and only help very rational subjects to succeed.

If you like being an emotional person, someone who really enjoys the thrill of pure feelings, your winning strategy will be focusing on your own improvement, adding competences, learning new subjects/sports/hobbies, improving your appearance, acquiring happiness and becoming a Perfect Partner.

This will bestow upon you an aura and charisma which will naturally put you above the masses.

The Earth is crowded with millions and millions of individuals of our species, but I am convinced that everybody will find, sooner or later, someone who fits their character and share their visions. Therefore…

You are entitled to be entirely yourself while looking for a partner, with a few nice additions and improvements, but always be yourself, heart & soul.

8.1 I NEED, YOU NEED, WE NEED

The principle of life states that every living being, be it plant or animal, will grow and develop harmoniously when cared for and loved.

As parents, we have the concept crystal clear in our minds... but when it's time to take care of a new relationship, we generally forget about it, and our subconscious makes sure that our needs are prioritized. It is not that we are egoistical and hysterical... it is a self-protection, survival instinct which we lose as soon we fall in love. But until then... we think and act only to reach one goal: the most complete fulfilment of our needs. These needs are absolutely subjective, they change with time, and have a sexual, spiritual, material and egoistic matrix. If you understand this atavistic mechanism, you can also prevent others perceiving that you are on a quest... how?

Keep a balance between Give & Take, but also between Offer & Demand

We have become acquainted with the first principle in a previous chapter. Offer & Demand is important in the first stage of a relationship, as you have to understand whether you and your prospective partner really want the same kind of experience from each other. Your two worlds are self-standing, still not connected, still not interdependent, and a lot of external factors can be responsible for sudden changes of the status quo. A *promising* situation can change into a *no more* one and vice versa. The first dating period is full of accidents, misunderstandings, and eventually you have to be very motivated in order to overcome these initial obstacles. We have to be realistic... we are not teenagers, and our evolution into adult single parents has turned us into quite complicated living beings. As long as we do not put an effort into trying to simplify our needs (love, stability, companionship, etc.) and express them truly and openly, the exchange of Offer & Demand will remain just as complicated. Overwhelming the other with requests, expectations and even with too much love, can be lethal for a relationship in the first stages. Anyway, in the outgoing and incoming of love articles (feelings, experiences, emotions etc.) *giving more* is allowed and can help a love relationship to progress and develop, while *expecting more* is to be handled with kid gloves.

If, after some time, you realize that your Give & Take account is in the red, aka negative, or very negative, start to question the very nature of your relationship. I need & YOU need can be very different from what WE need!

8.2 FEELING VS. ANALYZING

People who already have a marriage, or a long relationship behind them, are normally very cautious when it comes to investing energies into a new love story. Even when it's apparent that the time has come for letting love in, you might come face-to-face with the fear of suffering, losing valuable time, not being valued for what you are worth, not being understood...

We all want to be loved, understood and valued in a love relationship.

Also, those who appear very self-reliant and self-centred need YOUR appraisal. Now, in the first stage, when you get to know someone, you may be not in a position to express a feeling of love - except for those few times when it is *love at first sight*, but you can still communicate closeness and a genuine interest to this person. In doing so, you provide the much needed positive ground for a trusting relationship. Whether it will develop into a love relationship is still the big question!

Try to 'feel' your perspective partner— don't analyse them.

There is nothing more discouraging than feeling that the other person is 'observing' us instead of 'feeling' us.

Of course, you need to assess if your acquaintance is matching your own wishes, or at least most of them, especially revolving around concepts such as life vision, family, children, free time, role models, freedom, and so on. But the method you will use to assess their ability of being your Mr./Ms. Right shouldn't follow scientific paradigms, but rather the widest extent of your feelings and perceptions. Sometimes you go to the supermarket because you need to buy the milk, and you come home with milk, butter, bread, toilet tissue, avocados, cream and two kilograms of chocolate ice-cream. Sometimes, you think your ideal partner must have blue eyes, but after excluding three quarters of the entire world's male or female population, you go out with your brown eyed friend and you fall in love with them.

Analysing involves data collection and classification, according to given criteria. Feelings involve opening all of your senses and breathe, touch, smell, and listen to the person close to you.

Analysing is something for chemical laboratories... love wants magic!

Only a closer approach will let you really establish whether you are made for one another. Whatever falls under analysis, will lose its value, warmth and the very same target of every encounter: becoming intimate, a melding of souls and bodies.

Moreover, there are some men and women who will disclose their best, and show you the love they are truly capable of, only when you have opened the doors to your own heart and they feel comfortable enough to leave their emotional cocoon. With these people, a cold, distant dating approach doesn't work. Reserved, introverted, private people respond better to highly emotional experiences and approaches, than to conversations aimed at *discovering each other*. So feeling vs. analysing gains more points.

'Feeling' a prospective partner doesn't affect your objectivity; on the contrary, it adds insight into their spiritual and sensual world.

8.3 TIME FOR FALLING IN LOVE

Not long, not short, not medium...
Time is not a factor, nor an issue in falling
in love!

It can happen in one hour or might not happen in ten dates with the same person. Just relax, be yourself and take it easy.

I am for action, and action is life itself for me. *No Action = No Life. But... overdoing is a mistake*; there are times when you have to simply let time work for you and be patient... Quoting myself...

Let your projects be independent organisms.
They will develop their own beautiful
architecture.

If you are a starter, a mover, a provider, a friend of your family, of yourself and humanity, then you don't have to feel overwhelmed by action at all costs. Pretending to control the multiplicity and variety, along with the complexity of our world, is a utopia. We have to allow ourselves time to be just what we are: wonderful human beings. Most of us will be able to find a compromise between waiting and acting. There are sometimes very critical seconds, those when you decide whether *to call or not to call, to ask or not to ask, to push or not to push.*

Before every move forward with a prospective partner, ask yourself:

"How will he/she possibly understand what I am going to say/do?"

This must not affect your spontaneity, but rather give you additional time and wisdom to better understand and enter the psychology of your special person. Major damage in early relationships is caused by misunderstandings and emotional upheavals.

8.4 SYNCHRONICITY AND PATIENCE

Consider that what is wrong now, can be made right in a couple of hours or days, sometimes, even in *ages*.

> *Synchronicity is a science, and learning to manage time as a couple for the sake of harmony, can offer a number of advantages. Respecting the timing of your partner or prospective partner is critical.*

If your special one returns home very tired, you may want to wait until he/she has taken a shower, relaxed for a moment, gathered his/her thoughts, connected with your spiritual sphere, and then be ready to listen to you. Whether you tell him/her *"I love you"* or *"My dog has eaten your slippers"*, the concept is the same!

> *There is a right moment to tell and do everything! Just wait until the red lamp turns green.*

9 HOW TO PREVENT AND NEUTRALIZE ENERGY-SUCKING RELATIONAL STRESS

I am writing while my tablet PC is playing one of my favourite songs ever – 'All in Love is Fair', by Stevie Wonder. This old song used to be the soundtrack of a little romance featuring me and the ex-boyfriend of a real princess. It took some time for me to realize that my expectations were unrealistic. The guy was using me to forget his ex-girlfriend. I gave him back the self-confidence that the princess had taken away, but it was not enough. LOVE is not based on gratitude! Therefore, I did what I would do with any friend of mine – I helped him to find his own way to love happiness. I felt relieved... could relax and return to my single life without relational stress. It was a short story of reciprocated missed expectations.

Relational stress is the stress generated by conflicts and unfulfilled expectations inside the social and relationships area. It can badly affect self-confidence, damage the immune system and cause fatigue. Depression often results, with consequences to your overall performance.

Google search results for *stress* (in general) are about 689,000,000 hits. My only nephew, as he was four, used the word *stress* appropriately! But knowing the problem is not enough. You must tackle it and, although this kind of stress is sneakier and more deceptive than others, the means to prevent it and cope with it are simple and at hand!

Whatever the role you have in life (as head of a department, a friend, etc.), high relational expectations provide a great deal of stress. You expect to be appreciated for what you are or what you have done and expect that your colleagues, your friends, your siblings etc. will behave and respond according to your wishes, your own set of principles, beliefs and your projections. Disillusionment and conflicts (both internal and external) may result. You ruminate on why that person was so unfriendly to you, and in so doing, you consume positive life energy and produce StReSs. Now, while self-questioning is needed to improve your social awareness and skills, it must remain a limited process for you to grow and expand further.

Stop expecting that everyone likes you:
this is simply not possible!

No one in the history of mankind has ever been universally accepted as a good person, or a good leader, or a good friend, and so on. So who are you to expect that everybody likes you? There is some degree of narcissism in such a belief!

Your colleagues, your friends, your siblings, your prospective partner, etc. relate to you not only by the amount of positive effort you put into your relationships, but also by the ways they internalize you.

And how they internalize you is the product of their own personality, culture, set of principles and beliefs, the time in their life they are experiencing *now*, competition level, social background, religion, gender, age and also the product of their own changing expectations and needs concerning their relationship with you. Too many variables! In other words:

You are not entirely responsible for your relationships, nor can you do much to control them

Therefore, if you are sure you have done your best to make your relationships work (you were fair, loving, diligent, generous, respectful, responsible, trustworthy, and so on), that's enough! Further efforts to improve your interactions might be vain. ACCEPT THAT!

Downsizing your expectations about how you perform socially and your expectations about the feedback you'll get from social interactions, or some social interactions in particular, sets the ground for a stress-free social environment.

A less expectation-charged relationship usually works wonders; the people involved feel free to move inside it at their own pace and don't consider the issue of not meeting the standards of the other person as an eventual failure. Less conflicts are the positive side effect, as well as relaxed, light-hearted interactions.

Less Expectations → Less Conflicts → Less Stress

THE SIMPLE RULE: Reduce your relationship expectations and wait to see what happens. Should the problems/conflicts persist, put emotional (also physical, if needed) distance between you and the people who generate them. You are neither punishing nor banning these people from your life. Just claiming your right to your inner balance and to a happy and fulfilling life.

10 THE 10 FUNDAMENTALS FOR SURVIVING A DIVORCE / BREAKUP

I might look tired sometimes —I work around the clock in three languages, but everybody who knows me in person would tell you: "Roxy always looks happy!" I feel like the most fortunate lady in the world, despite the critical circumstances around my own divorce and post-divorce life.

1. You are a lizard.

You possess an amazing regeneration power, which you can use against any adverse circumstances. Like a lizard, you can heal your wounds and transform life's amputations into new and more interesting life chances.

2. Your Ex is not the archetype of his gender that is...not all men are 'Beeps' and not all women are 'Beeps'.

Talking or posting gender-discriminating material won't make the world better! Your ex was/is a shark? If you need to vent, vent against him/her, but leave other men and women outside of your personal war. Men don't like women who don't like men, as well as women don't like men who don't like women. We are mothers and fathers of a new generation who should live in a discriminations-free world. A general positive state of mind helps in coping with divorce and breakups in general. Complaining and fighting all the time against the other half of mankind doesn't!

3. Don't blame marriage or your past loving relationship for being the cause of your problems.

The matching with your ex was! Avoid this attitude, particularly in front of your children. They should have the right to experience for themselves how marriage is. You are an influencer in your children's life, and instilling prejudices against something, which is supposed to support the continuation of human life is clearly a no-go. We must accept the coexistence of good and bad. The good is the counterpart of bad, and vice-versa. There are good and bad apples, good and bad weather, good and bad marriages and loving relationships. Your next combo might be good and meet your highest expectations!

4. Create your future instead of demolishing your past.

Past is past, you've heard it thousands of times. Leave it behind you and focus on your dreams. A happy future for you and for your children, if any… that is what must occupy your thoughts and your time from now on!

5. If you consider yourself the most miserable person in the world, think about the fact that there are divorce and breakup circumstances which are even harder than yours to be coped with.

A few years ago, a mother of three told me that she was abandoned by her cheating husband as the youngest of their children was dying of blood cancer. She mastered divorce, the death of her son, the cheating, the solitude and the lack of a job wonderfully. She now works with and for children and has got a beautiful aura of positive energy, which makes her so special and loved.

6. Take care of your appearance.

The mirror is almost a mythological figure, as it is present in the oldest tales, often as an Alter Ego. There is more than an element of truth to the importance of looking good/well groomed - especially when you feel at your most frustrated, alone and lost. As it has been proven to enhance self-confidence.

7. Let your children be free...

...from preoccupations, accusations, and conflicts. Don't assign them responsibilities which don't belong to them, whatever their age. Even more traumatic than facing their family splitting up is the feeling that they are responsible for their parents' happiness. Don't play the victim or transfer your anxieties over to them. Don't have your wounds cured by your children; that could badly affect the harmonious growth and development of their personalities. Until they can trust in your strength, they will feel strong themselves. A virtuous cycle!

8. Pamper yourself.

Take time for your favourite activities or allow yourself something which you have long wished for and never dared to buy. Both spiritual and consumer-driven people find the word *pamper* one of the most attractive in the English dictionary. Use it!

9. Put emotional and physical distance between you and unmanageable feelings, people and problems.

Don't pretend to be able to master all situations and emotions at the same time. Minimize time and occurrence of painful meetings and conversations.

10. Time creates.

You can look at the same situation with different eyes after some time, because your appraisal, or its dynamics have changed. Don't give prompt answers or make important decisions as soon as a reaction is required from you - by the ex or his/her divorce-lawyer for example. Our mind needs time to adjust itself to new realities. More time if it's bad or difficult realities. We automatically start to make assessments, and if you decide before the process is ended (think of the rotating hourglass when software is loading on your PC) you risk making decisions based more on your *sense of frustration* than on your *common sense,* which can turn out to be detrimental for the positive course of future events.

MY LIFE–COACHING WORKBOOK

....

EXERCISE 1. GET RID OF SAD MEMORIES

Control and neutralize the ability of sad memories to affect your tranquillity and happiness, so that you never have to be afraid of looking back at your life. It can be an incident from as far back as childhood, or during your time at college, or any other segment of time when you were not 'happy'. It might have been a time when you were lacking in love, or friendship, or security, or money, or tranquillity, or a time when your right to exist without too many preoccupations and/or external pressures was under attack. It is important later on, to become reconciled with these events and times in your life. As unexpectedly as they come, you will learn to be able to control sad memories effectively. In essence: you will experience happier memories from now on. Enjoy it!

Please, start this challenge only when you know that nobody will disturb you for a minimum of 20 minutes.

TASK 1.

What was one of the saddest times in your life? Is there an object, *still present in your home*, which most connects you to this particular time in your past? It might be a picture, a book, a doll, a pair of shoes, etc. If you have a number of options, please choose an object which you can comfortably hold in your hands (not your old piano, for example). Go and grab this object.

Now hold it in your hands. Start walking around your environment, moving this object up and down in front of you, and making circles in the air with it, all the while keeping your eyes focused on the item. Let your mind wander free, don't exercise any control over your thoughts and reactions to your feelings. Accept what comes to your mind, and stay in motion for at least five minutes.

Then, as proof of what you've done, write down the following sentence: "I held my past in my hands and I moved it around as I wanted".

....

....

....

....

> *DID YOU KNOW? - What happened in your past is a fact, and a fact cannot be changed. How you experience these facts 'later' in your life is totally in your hands!*

"I have noticed that..."

....

....

....

....

....

TASK 2

Take a seat, while holding the same object in your hands. Touch it with your fingertips. Close your eyes if it helps you to enhance the touching sensation. Set your mind free, allowing your thoughts to come and go as they please. Keep holding the object for at least five minutes.

At the end of the time, establish whether the object is colder or warmer than before you started the exercise: remember – you can only answer 'colder' or 'warmer' (These are the only two available responses!). If you discover it's colder, got to your wardrobe and select a pullover/sweatshirt to wear; if it's warmer, go to the kitchen/bathroom sink and wash your hands in cold water to refresh them.

Then, as proof of what you've done, write down the following sentence: "*I can remove sad memories by sensing them outside of my body and neutralizing them*".

....

....

....

....

Repeat this exercise regularly, and you will become a master at externalizing, handling and neutralizing bad memories!

145

"I have noticed that..."

EXERCISE 2. ACCEPT THE BREAKUP AND BE HAPPY AGAIN

Parting from the ex-loved one is sometimes a real tragedy, especially if you are the weaker party (the one who earns less, who takes care of the children, who comes from a foreign country, and so on). Whether it's your partner's fault, yours, or the circumstances surrounding both of you, your relationship has suffered so much that perhaps it can no longer be healed. This turns out to be particularly true, if you have already taken all the necessary steps to save your union, but everything you've tried has failed miserably (for example, family counselling, vacations and activities meant to regain closeness with your partner, and so on). Here, you will learn how to accept the end of your love relationship and be happy again!

TASK 1

Accepting the breakup implies abandoning a lot of recurring (not to say obsessive) thoughts – below are some examples:

- "Why does he/she behave in this manner and not in the other, what I think is the right way?"
- "Who is my ex with now, instead of being at work as they said they would be?"
- "What can I do to change and improve this situation for the better?"

Write down the following sentences and then read them aloud (I advise you to repeat this task, at least once a day for ten days):

1. The character, psychological problems, social background, mentality, and the lack of principles in my ex-partner are no longer my business. Full stop!

....

....

....

2. The life my ex-partner now lives is no longer my business. Full stop!

....

....

....

3. Notwithstanding any positive efforts made to change the situation, my loving relationship was lacking the essential elements to make it a happy one. Full stop!

....

....

....

Then, as proof of what you've done, write down the following sentence: *"I have stopped thinking about my ex and will now focus on myself."*

....

....

....

....

DID YOU KNOW? - Acceptance is like a breeze inside your head, refreshing your brain and allowing more space and power to convert your future plans into action.

"I have noticed that..."

TASK 2

Ruminating on how sick your loving relationship, your (ex)-partner and the situation were/are, is time, health, and mind consuming: a STRONG stress factor! You have divorced/parted, something 40% and more of the people around you have already experienced. You have lost a partner who was not the best person for you. Something very important, in any long-lasting relationship is no longer there. This something can be respect, love, dedication, engagement, or all of the above. You know better than any other person on earth why it happened, what that missing something was. Without its essential elements, you get an imperfect surrogate—not a real love relationship! There are a lot of happy couples, who after twenty years together, still care for each other. You deserve to be happy too.

> Go into a crowded place (shopping mall, park, busy street) and locate and count ten 'OLD, HAPPY couples'.

Then, as proof of what you've done, write down the following sentence: "One day, I will also be in a happy and harmonious relationship with my future partner and it might last forever!"

....

....

....

DID YOU KNOW? - Human beings respond to natural rhythms, as do any other living beings; like falling leaves, dead partnerships must be replaced to give room for beautiful new forms of relationships and love.

"I have noticed that..."

TASK 3

Don't believe that your marriage/relationship was 'good' just because, apparently, your everyday routine worked. Don't argue that no relationship is perfect! That is the soup some parents have served to their children, mostly daughters, for centuries, in order to lower their expectations while they are hunting high and low for a spouse. A bad marriage was once presumed to be a lot better than no marriage at all, and I'm sure that even today, in many cultures and subcultures, this concept continues to produce people who are resigned to being unhappy for a lifetime.

What about your real wants, your need for closeness and time together?

Make a very orderly and complete *PARTNERSHIP WISH LIST*, including of all your *WISHES* for your future relationship. While writing this list down, feel how wonderful it is, to be free of a bad partnership and finally able to live the relationship of your dreams.

> *Read your Partnership Wish List from now on, at least once a day, for a couple of weeks.*

Determination in what you want to achieve is important, particularly in love.

Then, as proof of what you've done, write down the following sentence: "*The List is done!*"

DID YOU KNOW? - You must archive your failed marriage. Accept the end. Don't fight against it! Let a healing calmness flow inside you.

"I have noticed that..."

EXERCISE 3. HAPPY PARENTING

Do you wish to be more satisfied with the time you spend with your children and achieve a stronger bond with them?

TASK 1

Sometimes parents are so engaged in providing their children with all they need, so focused on their role of life-guides and educators that they forget to genuinely enjoy parenting. Look back at your last seven days and mentally list all the things you did with your children, including the times when you were just assisting them in doing something like homework, or taking them to swimming lessons. Think about whether you perceive each of these activities as:

1. *Frustrating* - i.e. you were bored, feeling like your child/ren's personal servant/taxi driver. A to-do-list entry.

2. *Accomplishing* - i.e. you accomplished your parental role and you were satisfied by it, but you wouldn't say you had much fun doing it; or

3. *Fun* - you personally (not as a result of the joy reflected by your children) enjoyed doing this activity and you can't wait to have such a great time with your children again!

4. Done?

Once you've thought through these situations and discovered if your time with your children has been mainly frustrating, accomplishing or fun, write down the following sentence: *"I can measure the degree of satisfaction I get from my time spent with my children"*.

....

....

....

....

DID YOU KNOW? - Happier parents are better parents and have happier children. Children are sensitive to parents' positive changes and respond accordingly.

"I have noticed that..."

....

....

....

....

....

....

....

....

TASK 2

You have already completed your first task, great! Now wait 3 days before going to Task 2. Why? This is the technical time your mind requires to get acquainted and work best with new important concepts and goals. Observe yourself while spending time with/for your children, and mentally *measure* your degree of contentment/satisfaction in the way you learned to do in TASK 1. Never forget that your goal is to become a happier parent; think only about this now and the beautiful side effects which will come as a positive consequence. I know that you can't wait to move on to the next step, but please, only go on after you have accomplished this task. I wish you a good time with your children. See you in three days!

As proof of taking this 3-day break to measure your degree of happiness/contentment, write down the following sentence: "*I am aware of the degree of satisfaction I get, from spending time with my children.*"

DID YOU KNOW? - Awareness is fundamental to personal development and growth, the very starting point for every successful life change!

TASK 3

Welcome to Task 3! Now that you are more sensitive to your own personal needs concerning your relationship with your children, you can start to work on improving your degree of satisfaction as a parent. *Switch on this new attitude in your mind: 50/50!*

For example: if before you were doing 2 activities per week revolving only around your children, now for 2 activities per week you should take them to whatever place they feel happiest to go to - parties, sports games etc., and 2 times per week, you should do something together that *you* like - for example, going to the theatre, visiting a museum, gardening, bird-watching, etc. Now please repeat this affirmation to yourself, 5 TIMES:

"I have found a balance between the time I spend with my children to meet their wishes, and the time I spend with my children to meet my wishes."

As proof that you have completed this task, write down the following sentence: *"50% of the time I spend with my children, will match up with my own wishes."*

DID YOU KNOW? - Children's most recurrent answer to the question, "What do you like most about your parents?" is this response: "When Mom/Dad plays with me." → *Togetherness and Fun!*

"I have noticed that..."

TASK 4

The concepts and mechanisms which you internalize through this exercise will help you to achieve higher levels of satisfaction in all of your interactions with your children in the future. But in the here and now, you start by processing bigger time clusters, those involving your free time with your children.

Divide one (or more if needed) A4 sheets of paper in equal parts, by drawing a cross through the centre. Then, write on top of each section, in capital letters, one *favourite* hobby or activity and repeat the procedure for the other sections. Finished? Don't put this list away, because you will need it for your next task.

Then, as proof of what you've done, write down the following sentence: *"I have made a list including all my favourite activities and hobbies.*

....

....

....

....

DID YOU KNOW? - Doing what you like most, even when you encounter difficulties, makes you happy, enhances your senses and improves your immune system.

TASK 5

Parents who renounce their dreams to serve only their family's needs, are not only less happy, but they are also not loved any more than parents who reserve their right to personal happiness and fulfilment. The perception of your *giving* in terms of time and dedication, is different from a child's point of view. Under each entry on the list you created in Task Four, list items you'll need, aimed at making it a fun experience for your children; don't forget to adapt the requirements to their age, also remembering to keep safety in mind.

Example: RECREATIONAL BOAT FISHING

✓ with Macy, 6 years old – life preserver and vest, children's fishing rod, dog, Barbie, snacks, a prize for the fishing exercise;

and

✓ with Tom, 17 years old - life preserver and vest, his girlfriend, camera.

What you have completed is the Reference Table for your future activities together.

Now, I want you to wait until the following day before moving forward! You need to sleep on the information you've included in your Reference Table.

Done?

The following morning, when you've had the opportunity to mull over your list and add anything extra that you've thought about overnight, write down this sentence: *"I have turned all of my favourite hobbies and activities into fun and safe activities for all of us."*

....

....

....

....

DID YOU KNOW? - Shared happy experiences create deeper bonds than gratitude alone!

"I have noticed that..."

....

....

....

....

....

....

....

....

....

TASK 6

You may not have realized it yet, but this challenge has already produced positive changes in the perception of your role as a parent and in your attitudes. You are going to turn your wishes into real, beautiful experiences for you and your children.

I bet you have included at least one activity requiring no particular planning and preparation, which is compatible with your children's schedule and can be done right away. If not... no problem.

The first thing you must do is ANNOUNCE the activity. This is very important: don't give them the opportunity to refuse... that is... to AVOID. Rather than say *"Would you like to..."*, instead simply and with lot of self-confidence say: *We're doing [the activity]"*. If you want to make the announcement more interesting, you could describe what you are intending to do, leaving some room for a surprise - even when your children are twenty years old, a good surprise is always a good surprise.

Then, as proof of what you've done, write down the following sentence: *"I have announced to my children what activity we are going to do next."*

....

....

....

....

DID YOU KNOW? - Some children show little enthusiasm at the prospect of doing something new or different until they are actually 'experiencing' the activity.

"I have noticed that..."

TASK 7

And… here we are! I hope you are going to explore a world of new and exciting possibilities as far as your time with your children is concerned! But for now, we limit our attention to the one you have announced. I trust 100% in your capacity to make it a great, fun experience for you all, even if it's only baking chocolate muffins together or golfing (if baking and golfing happened to be included in your Reference Table).

Now go and do what you have announced to be the first activity in the previous task. In case you have limited time available, set a timer, but don't continuously check your watch. *Don't forget: Togetherness & Fun!*

This activity is designed for you to achieve maximum satisfaction from the time you spend with your children. This means that after you have completed the preparation work you HAVE TO RELAX AND ENJOY IT LIKE A CHILD!

Then, as proof of what you've done, write down the following sentence: *"I had fun and got a lot of satisfaction from the time I spent doing this activity with my children"*.

....

....

....

....

DID YOU KNOW? - There is always room for improvement. You will choose to stop doing an activity only if you see that it is 'repeatedly' creating discontentment

"I have noticed that..."

EXERCISE 4. MASTER THE FIRST DATE! FOR WOMEN

Normally, I offer gender-neutral coaching. But clichés make life difficult on your first date, when you have to play to all your assets. So here is a fun challenge to GREATLY improve your results.

TASK 1

The man you have been waiting for is late? It doesn't mean he's going to stand you up. He's just late! Don't get nervous about your first date because of unimportant reasons. For example, if your hair insists on hanging over your forehead and refuses to go back in place; or the flu has left you with a bit of hoarseness in your throat, and you feel more like a frog than a princess; or you are in the midst of your menstrual cycle. (God, that really *is* a problem… ahem this is, well… actually, this is a sign you shouldn't rush into more than is sensible on a first date!)

On your first date, yes, it's important that you look good but even more so – that you look CALM.

So here is your task, to be completed before the official 'first date'. Choose the right outfit, style your hair and use *some* make-up (to *reduce* imperfections rather than to *highlight* perfections); in other words, prepare as you would do for your first date. Now go out for the evening and enter FIVE different venues, which are crowded with men. In each venue, repeat the following actions:

While wearing your best smile, approach the man you find most attractive in the room and ask him the following question: *"Can you please tell me who is the owner/boss/coach here? I need some information."* While he's answering your question, look directly into his eyes, maintaining eye contact the whole time. Then smile again, while saying *"Thank you very much for your help!"* If you think the exchange has gone well, you can prolong the conversation. The longer you talk, the more successfully you are accomplishing this task!

Then, as proof of what you've done, write down the following sentence: *"I have trained my self-confidence by approaching five very attractive men."*

....

....

....

....

DID YOU KNOW? - Men don't like too much makeup or too many colours, unless you only intend to flirt. Look at how many colours men combine together - and you'll realize I am right.

"I have noticed that..."

....

....

....

....

TASK 2

He sits there, in front of you, and he doesn't say a thing... because you have been talking all the time! Please, ask him questions about his work and his favourite hobby, and wait... *wait*. Silences can be very nice, too. You can understand a lot of things from how a person masters a period of silence.

Think of the person you are going to date. If no one is on your horizon, imagine your Mr. Right! Write down ten prospective questions regarding his private life; ten questions regarding his job; ten general subject questions (hobbies/tastes/sports). *Learn these thirty questions* by heart, and ensure your voice is calm, fluid and natural when you practice them. Call a male friend or colleague, and either over the phone or in person, ask him the thirty questions, trying not to interrupt or disturb him until he is finished answering each one. Then you can comment, if you wish. Look him in the eyes and show interest. Don't measure the success of your questions on this TEST FRIEND however: everybody is different.

Then, as proof of what you've done, write down the following sentence: *"I have practiced my thirty questions with a friend"*.

....

....

....

....

DID YOU KNOW? - If you reveal more than half of the length of your legs beneath your skirt, then he might think you want an 'all you can eat' first date. Is this the message you want to give him?

"I have noticed that..."

TASK 3

It is absolutely imperative, that you do not tell your date to give up something (from his smoking habit to his favourite hobby) on your first date. *("It is not healthy to smoke", or "What the heck? Free climbing can be really dangerous. You'd be better to do a safer sport, maybe play golf instead).* Men react as if being zapped by high voltage to any kind of constraints being put upon them. You are adults, who have led past lives, and should he also be a divorcee, he is currently enjoying his life more than ever - no one is limiting him now! So if you don't come to terms with his hobbies and smoking habits or whatever else he may do that you don't like, you had better let him go, rather than test his abilities to adapt to your wishes.

List aspects you cannot tolerate in a man – those that you could never come to terms with (i.e. rude language, uneducated). Evaluate these disturbing factors by measuring your level of rejection. The more you evaluate now, the better can you master your date 'in person'.

Then, as proof of what you've done, write down the following sentence: *"I know I cannot change a man's habits, therefore I either accept them or reject them outright."*

....

....

....

....

DID YOU KNOW? - First dates often show later a certain number of other peculiarities like little manias, recurring habits, which add up to your list of cons.

"I have noticed that..."

TASK 4

Camaraderie with men is good for them to have within their friendships with other men, but you are not going out with this guy because you want to be his friend. Are you? There is nothing more demoralizing for men with erotic intentions towards a woman than to have her tell him how he feels in his own pants. You are a woman, and he is a man. And you are on your first date. Your understanding of a man's world is good? Terrific! Cool! Nice! But don't tell him how he should look and smile at the amazing looking blonde who is drinking two seats over. This is date suicide.

If you are interested in him, don't send false messages of non-interest. Don't test him in this way or that way, to discover whether he is interested. Most guys are not tuned in to Radio Psychic. Their thoughts are straightforward and simple, so do the same and you will win their heart!

To confirm that you have understood this concept, write down the following: *"I won't behave like his best friend, but like his best date, and I won't test his interest in me through testing his interest."*

....

....

....

....

DID YOU KNOW? - As a matter of fact, the first date is actually a test, but keep it to yourself! Men don't like to be analysed, especially on first dates

"I have noticed that..."

....

....

....

....

....

....

....

....

....

....

....

....

....

....

....

....

....

TASK 5

Let me share a couple more words of advice with you from one girl to another. Pssst, come closer.

Guys are usually threatened like lambs being followed by ravenous wolves when you ask the question: *"Is marriage somewhere in your future plans?"* Unfortunately, even in the event that the man is well intentioned regarding marrying sooner or later - and maybe he is dating you because he does want to settle down (again) – but this question will raise his wild, atavistic fears and switch on a 'red alert alarm' in his head. You can be nice, intelligent, interesting, sexy, and cute, and have totally natural, amazing D-cup breasts; but he will always see you as the wolf that wants to eat him. Don't ask this question – ever – on a first date!

Say this sentence, out loud, five times: *"I will enjoy his company and his stories and try not to think too far ahead."* Repeat it aloud again, shortly before you meet your first date and try to remain as light-hearted as possible during the entire experience. Good Luck!

Then, as proof of what you've done, write down the following sentence: *"I will enjoy his company and his stories and try not to think too far ahead."*

DID YOU KNOW? - The first date is designed to get to know another person, not to make future plans with him. Focus on the person. The rest will come!

"I have noticed that..."

EXERCISE 5. MASTER THE FIRST DATE! *FOR MEN*

Normally, I offer gender-neutral coaching. But clichés make life difficult on your first date, when you have to play all your assets. So here is a fun challenge to GREATLY improve your results.

TASK 1

The majority of women on their first date will be making a 3D portrait of you as a whole (your intellect, body, and character, and well... yes, sometimes also the balance of your equity account and how many Ferraris you own). While talking, they are scanning and weighing up all the information you give and looking for key features. One of these is *balance*. Spending the first forty-five minutes of your first date only talking about your spinning workouts and your spinning weekends, or any other activity or hobby that is extremely time-consuming is A HUGE MISTAKE!

Sit in front of a big mirror, and using a timer, talk nonstop about yourself and your life vision for twenty minutes. At the end of this exercise, write down in time percentages, how long you have talked about each section of your vision. Take notes of what you missed out on – and that might be important - because you gave priority to some subjects and didn't cover others.

Then, as proof of what you've done, write down the following sentence: "*I will keep my conversation varied and balanced from the very beginning.*"

DID YOU KNOW? - Women, especially in their 30s & over are programmed by nature to find good fathers, but have also learned to find good lovers. Are you a hot Provider?

"I have noticed that..."

TASK 2

Women like generous men, regardless of role divisions or financial possibilities. Leaving the restaurant where you had your first date and only paying for your share of the meal, is a NO GO! The woman in front of you might be the equivalent of Ivana Trump in monetary value, and able to submerge you in gold if she felt the desire to do so, but the fact remains that women like polite men who treat them to a nice time and are willing to pay for the first date. They will forgo this polite approach only if the man can abundantly compensate for this lack of manners with a number of other qualities. If you are as good looking as Michael Fassbender, as intelligent as Einstein, or as funny as Jim Carrey, then you can suggest paying separately at the restaurant! If not, you should set out with the intentions of paying for your date's first dinner with you.

Set your budget for your first date. You must impress, but don't go beyond your capabilities. Avoid fast food restaurants unless you're under twenty! Pay and forget about it; don't continually highlight your generosity. Is that clear?

To prove that you know what to do, write down the following sentence: *"I will offer to pay the restaurant bill on our first date, because I want to assert my strong, providing, masculine role."*

179

DID YOU KNOW? - Stating your firm belief that a prenuptial agreement is a warranty for finding a 'pure love' on your first date can be honest, but lethal.

"I have noticed that..."

TASK 3

Most men think that taking it slowly is what women want. FALSE!

On your first date it means: smiling; touching her hand for short, casual caresses; saying something nice about her hair/outfit/voice/eyes/intelligence/sensitivity or beauty, while maintaining eye contact; listening; asking questions about her job/family/hobbies/plans for the future/life vision and principles; using warm words in the conversation – *warm words* such as love/feelings/thoughts/relationships friendships, family and children – and what's more, you can connect to your heart without being afraid of being considered a softy. Be a gentleman but always walk & sit close to her; and check her comfort level. Does she look nervous? If the answer is yes, slow down. The rule is "*be respectful, but assertive*".

So here is your task, to be undertaken before you go out on your first date with a new woman. Go out, smile and speak to five women who you don't know but find attractive and say something nice about them. Observe their reaction and continue the conversation (if any) as long as they do not appear annoyed and seem interested in continuing the conversation.

Then, as proof of what you've done, write down the following sentence: "*I managed to speak to five, previously unknown, attractive women without annoying them.*"

DID YOU KNOW? - You will fail to catch your butterfly in the net if you are distracted and slow. Special interest for a special woman? Make it clear & fast!

"I have noticed that..."

TASK 4

Everyone expects something different when starting a date. I assume you are serious about wishing to start a loving relationship with someone. If that is the case, your first date must contain the seeds for something solid. *Trust* is one of these seeds in every relationship. Most women on a first date use it as a very strict selection criterion. Therefore, tell the truth, whatever you say and yet keep your date *light and fresh*! If trust was an issue in your past, no problem… you can be an angel in your future!

Divide a sheet of paper into two columns: on the left side, list questions you would find uncomfortable or sensitive to answer. Then in the right hand column, you need to write down the relevant answers. Please give yourself enough time to think over your responses, and be true with yourself. Should your nice date ask one or more of those uncomfortable questions, you should now be able to master the situation and reply without feeling so uneasy.

Write the following sentence, once you have completed the task:

"I am prepared to truthfully answer the most sensitive questions about myself, without embarrassment."

....

....

....

....

DID YOU KNOW? - Details which could directly affect the life of your future partner should be shared ASAP: family status, chronic diseases, pending criminal charges, if any.

"I have noticed that..."

TASK 5

After you pay the restaurant bill, if she is indeed your butterfly, propose something to do right afterwards (such as a coffee, or visit a music club). If she doesn't accept, extend a further invitation for an all-day second date. You will have more time to get to know each other.

On the other hand, nothing is compulsory except good manners - even when, with a second deeper glance at her cleavage, you discover that she is filling her bra with toilet paper (not even those spongy lift supports women use to enhance their breast size!). Disillusionment is common, especially if you have met your date on the internet and she has photo-shopped all of her pictures. If you aren't interested in pursuing a second date, don't tell her "*I will phone you.*" Just say "*Good bye.*"

Prepare a list with at least ten entries including local sights, bars, weekend possibilities, parks in the area and any other exciting entertaining activity intended for use as an after-date.

Once you have made this list, write down the following sentence:

"I can propose more than ten interesting activities to do together after our first-date."

....

....

....

....

DID YOU KNOW? - If there is a thing women go mad for, it's a guys´ INITIATIVE. The more proactive you are, the more successful you'll be.

"I have noticed that..."

EXERCISE 6. PRESERVE AND STRENGTHEN YOUR IDENTITY

In a world where you are required to perform twenty-four hours a day, it sometimes happens that you forget WHO you really are. This affects your HAPPINESS more than you can imagine! On the way to success in a job, with your family or in a social arena, you should never have to feel detached from your own identity/self or let others always have the last word regarding how you are, feel and what you wish.

Please begin this exercise only when you know for certain that nobody will disturb you for a minimum of 20 minutes.

What you will need: *a timer.*

1.   Read the instructions all the way to the end of each task;
2.   Set your timer for five minutes;
3.   Begin the task.

When the alarm rings, you can stop if you are finished; if you have not completed the task, you can continue – take all the time you need.

TASK 1

Go to the centre of the room and CLOSE YOUR EYES. Feel your body's presence, physically, in the centre of the room and after you have got it, visualize the walls as if they are collapsing and falling down, letting you see the outside world around you.

KEEP YOUR EYES CLOSED.

What do you 'see'?

As proof that you have completed the Task, please write down a *short description of what you have seen around yourself, after the walls have collapsed.*

....

....

....

....

....

....

....

DID YOU KNOW? - People insert into your mind and your heart, thoughts and feelings which don't belong to you. Listen, watch, and read but always remain critical.

"I have noticed that..."

....

....

....

....

TASK 2

Originality is created by typical characteristics which make you DIFFERENT from other people. Originality doesn't always imply popularity but it's your way of preserving your identity and say to the world *how you feel* and *what you are*.

Please write down *some characteristics about yourself, starting from your earliest childhood memories* - for example: You could draw the nicest butterflies in first grade; As a teenager, you had a special haircut and colour, different to your friends; At work, you are the one who always discovers bugs, etc.

....

....

....

....

....

DID YOU KNOW? - In your effort to please, you may have left your originality in the waiting room. Are you really happy without it? Go and get it!

"*I have noticed that...*"

....

....

....

TASK 3

1. Examine your present job and your relationships (family-friends-partner) as you were a reconnaissance plane flying above them. Collect as many impressions as you can, then…

2. …make a list of the biggest dreams you have for your life, but which remain unfulfilled.

....

....

....

....

....

When you are finished creating the list, *put an "I" before each dream when it was your choice or fault that it remains unfulfilled, and an "O" when it is unfulfilled due to putting it off in favour of other people's opinions/needs.*

DID YOU KNOW? - You lose your best opportunities in life by accommodating others too much or fostering somebody else´s life chances more than your own. Make YOUR own dreams come true!

"I have noticed that…"

....

....

TASK 4

Preserving your identity means also defending yourself from any attempt by third parties to reduce, change or somehow manipulate your way of thinking and wishing in order for them to obtain advantages.

Your role in the world is interactive. You don't only receive and perform, but also receive and react. Now, visualize your *opponents* (people, institutions, radio, internet, TV etc.) as a player in a table tennis (ping pong) match. You receive the ball, and you hit the ball back.

> *YOU CHARGE THE BALL WITH...*
> *YOUR OWN ENERGY,*
> *YOUR OWN SPEED,*
> *YOUR OWN DIRECTION.*
> *AND WHEN YOU ARE TIRED...*
> *YOU ASK FOR A TIME-OUT!*

Write down *the three last times when you did something just to please* (your boss, your partner, your children or whoever else) *and not because you were convinced that it was right or also in your best interests.*

1.

2.

3.

Then write down your Alternative version, in which you do what was best for yourself.

1. A

2. A

3. A

DID YOU KNOW? - Strong Identity: visualize your body in the centre of the universe and opponents as ping pong players. Don't forget to ask for time-out and go for your dreams!

"I have noticed that..."

TO MY READER

Dear Reader,

I hope you enjoyed "IF YOU WANT YOU CAN FLY." I got so many letters from fans thanking me for my books. I love feedbacks and, candidly, you are the reason why I write.

I am dedicated to helping people live a happy and more fulfilled life, so tell me what you liked, what you loved, even what you hated and whether my book has positively impacted your state of mind and/or your life. I'd love to hear from you! You can write me at author.rossana-condoleo@rossanacondoleo.com and visit me on the web at www.rossanacondoleo.com.

Finally, I have to ask you a favour. If you are so inclined, I'd love a review of "IF YOU WANT YOU CAN FLY." Loved it, hated it — I'd just enjoy your feedback. As you may have gleaned from my books, reviews can be tough to come these days. You, the Reader, have the power now to make or break a book. If you have the time, on my homepage www.rossanacondoleo.com you find all my books and their links to the bookstores where you can leave you review.

Thank you so much for reading "IF YOU WANT YOU CAN FLY" and for spending your precious time with me.

I wish you all the very best for your future life. May everything that you do make you happy and **FLY**.

Love your way

Rossana Condoleo

www.ingramcontent.com/pod-product-compliance
Lightning Source LLC
Chambersburg PA
CBHW071739120626
46550CB00002B/587